"Precious in the sight of the Lord is the death of his saints."

—Psalm 115:14

St. Margaret Clitherow
"The Pearl of York"
c. 1553-1586
Canonized in 1970 as one of the
Forty Martyrs of England and Wales

ST. MARGARET CLITHEROW

'THE PEARL OF YORK"

Wife, Mother,
Martyr for the Catholic Faith
Under Queen Elizabeth I

By

Margaret T. Monro

"Every one therefore that shall con-
fess me before men, I will also confess
him before my Father who is in
heaven." —Matthew 10:32

TAN BOOKS AND PUBLISHERS, INC.
Rockford, Illinois 61105

Nihil Obstat: Reginald Phillips, S. T. L.
                    Censor Deputatus

Imprimatur: E. Morrogh Bernard
                    Vicar General
                    Westminster
                    October 30, 1945

Published in 1946 under the title *Blessed Margaret Clitherow* by Burns Oates and Washbourne, London.

Retypeset and republished in 2003 by TAN Books and Publishers, Inc.

ISBN 0-89555-771-1

Cover illustration and frontispiece: Portrait of St. Margaret Clitherow by David R. Perez, Jr. based on an old woodcut. Portrait copyright © 2003 by TAN Books and Publishers, Inc.

Printed and bound in the United States of America.

TAN BOOKS AND PUBLISHERS, INC.
P.O. Box 424
Rockford, Illinois 61105

2003

"I am fully resolved in all things touching my Faith, which I ground upon *Jesu* Christ, and by Him I steadfastly believe to be saved . . . and by God's assistance I mean to live and die in the same Faith; for if an angel come from heaven, and preach any other doctrine than we have received, the Apostle biddeth us not believe him."
—*St. Margaret Clitherow* (page 8).

"I die for the love of my Lord *Jesu!*"
—*St. Margaret Clitherow* (page 83).

Statue of St. Margaret Clitherow
in St. Wilfrid's Church, York.

CONTENTS

"Jam hiems transiit, imber-
abiit, et recessit: surge, amica
mea, et veni." —Off. Parv.
B. Mariæ ad Vesperas.

St. Margaret Clitherow

"For winter is now past, the rain is over and gone.
Arise, my love, and come."
(Vespers of the *Little Office of the Blessed Virgin Mary*).

How We Know about Her

MARGARET Clitherow, wife of a York butcher, was put to death for her religion under Queen Elizabeth in 1586. She is sometimes called "the protomartyr of her sex in England," though strictly the title should go to Blessed Margaret Pole [1471-1541], who was executed about forty years earlier, under Henry VIII. Yet we may allow that Margaret Clitherow has a glamour all her own, which imprints her image on the minds of men. Her gaiety and courage, her wit and her charity, combine to produce a very special flavor. That she should also be the mother of a young family adds poignancy to the story. It has been remarked that, like the protomartyr of England, St. Alban [d. 304], she died for the "crime" of harboring priests.

We know her with unusual intimacy because her "ghostly father"—we should now say her spiritual director—wrote an account of her within three months of her death. He was Mr. John Mush, a seminary priest who began his studies at the College in Douay, but in 1579 was sent to finish his course in Rome. He probably came on the English mission in 1582 or 1583, so that he knew Margaret Clitherow only for the last three or four years of her life—though it is always possible that he had come across her before he went abroad to study for the priesthood. What he tells us of her finished holiness makes a singularly moving picture.

At two points, however, Father Mush had to depend on the testimony of others. He was nearly caught in Margaret's house when she was arrested, and being in hiding himself, he was not present at her trial. But he collected the story of her last days from eye-witnesses and had the sense to write it down all but unadorned. From her arrest to her death, his story moves with the tense sureness of great drama. It is clear, too, that Father Mush had in his mind the greatest of all dramas: in scene after scene, he brings out points of likeness to the Passion of Our Lord.

And Father Mush also had to consult witnesses about the early part of her life. Here, however, he could not venture to be too explicit, simply because the story concerned people still alive. The dead could suffer no further harm from the malice of men, but it would never do to let the Government get a hint as to what priest reconciled Margaret to the Church, or what layfolk helped her in her difficulties. Therefore, the early part of his book is mainly a character study or portrait, very skillfully and delicately drawn, but less enthralling than the last chapters, which tell of her sufferings and death.

Father Mush's narrative is called *A True Report*

of the Life and Martyrdom of Mrs. Margaret Clitherow. The most important copy extant must have been made from a copy written by Father Mush within three months of Margaret's death. Another copy, now in the possession of the Bar Convent at York, must be somewhat later, since it gives details of people who had died in the interval and whom, therefore, the first copy had passed over in silence. The earlier version has long been in the possession of the family of Middleton, of Middleton Park and Stockeld; and this was printed in 1877 by Father John Morris, S.J., in the Third Series of his *Troubles of Our Catholic Forefathers*. The Bar Convent copy had been printed in 1849 by W. Nicholson. It is on Father Morris's edition that the present book is mainly based, since it contains valuable research into the Middleton and Clitherow families and into the affairs of the recusants* of York during Margaret's lifetime. The quotations in this book, unless otherwise stated, are from Father Morris's edition, mainly from Father Mush's narrative, occasionally from other documents printed in the same volume.

The dates of Margaret's life are not quite certain. Two we definitely know. She was married on July 1, 1571, and she died on March 25, 1586, a day which was Lady Day [Feast of the Annunciation] by the Old Style and Good Friday by the

---

*Recusant—an English Catholic who refused to attend the Protestant prayer service.—*Publisher*, 2003.

New.[1] Father Mush evidently felt it significant that her death should thus coincide with our remembrance both of the Incarnation and of the Crucifixion. At the time of her death, she had been a Catholic twelve years, and had a boy of fourteen. The age of this boy, Henry, suggests that Father Mush makes her rather too young in saying that she was "about thirty" at the time of her death, for she can hardly have been married when only fifteen. A beautiful woman in her early thirties, with a clear complexion and great physical vitality, may well have looked younger than her actual age. If we put her at eighteen at the time of her marriage, twenty-one at her conversion, and thirty-three at her death, we get a workable framework of dates which fits all the known facts. Her birth then would have been about 1553, during the reign of Mary Tudor, making her five years old when Elizabeth came to the throne.

Another source of information is, of course, the general history of Elizabeth's reign. Reading between Father Mush's lines, we can fit many slight touches into the framework of history and thus see more of their significance. To do this with

---

1. Four years before Margaret Clitherow's death, Pope Gregory XIII had reformed the Calendar, but since England was a Protestant country it did not accept calendar correction from Rome. Not until 1754 did England adopt the Gregorian calendar, so that in regard to all dates between 1582 and 1754 historians have to give them according to the two different methods of computation, that is, Old and New Style.

any thoroughness would take a book two or three times the length of this. But by keeping the following facts in mind, the reader may be able to get his own bearings without much further explanation.

English Catholics under Queen Elizabeth I

First and foremost, Elizabeth came to the throne in 1558 as a Catholic princess reigning over a Catholic people. At that date, the vast majority of English people were Catholic, and wished to remain Catholic. This does not mean that they were ready to make great sacrifices to retain their Faith. They simply did not understand that sacrifice could be necessary to keep something that had been theirs for nine hundred years. They had already seen, within their own lifetime, no fewer than three changes of religion, all of them short-lived. Faced with a fourth change, they shrugged their shoulders and waited for it to blow over like the rest. Moreover, the confiscation of nearly all the country's educational endowment had led to a great increase of ignorance. The England of Elizabeth was thus an easily bamboozled country. And the bamboozling was in the hands of a political genius who made the most of his opportunity. That genius was William Cecil, later Lord Burghley, Elizabeth's chief minister and the real architect of the Reformation in England. A paper probably drawn up by him, before the Queen was crowned or Parliament had met, lays down the methods by which the country's religion was to be changed. It is called *A Device for the Alteration of Religion*, and it recognizes frankly that the English were not going to like having their religion altered. Cecil therefore went about the job very skillfully, in order that the people might never appreciate what was happening, and so never offer effective resistance.

The story of Elizabeth's first thirty years, then, is the story of how the English people slowly woke up to the fact that, if they wanted their Faith, they must be ready to suffer for it. Before they woke up, the opportunity had in fact been lost. But of course people could not know that at the time, as we know it, for we can scrutinize the secret documents and confidential reports on which the Government acted.

During the first ten years of Elizabeth's reign, the country acquiesced in a stunned sort of way. This was partly because Elizabeth was expected to have as short a reign as her brother and sister—and then the next heir was a Catholic. People sat tight, expecting the Catholic religion to come back without exertion on their part. But when after ten years the Queen seemed as healthy as ever, while all traces of the Old Religion were rapidly disappearing, there was a natural disposition to reconsider the whole situation.

The second ten years of the reign, then, was a period of widespread restiveness and revolt. They open with the flight into England of Mary Queen of Scots, the Catholic heir to the throne, whose presence sent a tremor through the country. The next year, 1569, saw the Rising in the North, not to put Mary on the throne, but to deliver Elizabeth from the bad counsellors who were misleading her about her subjects' wishes. In 1570 came the Papal excommunication of Elizabeth, giving color to the severity with which the Rising in the North had been crushed. It was in ground thus ploughed by suffering that the Catholic spiritual revival took root and spread.

That spiritual revival had begun among the English exiles on the Continent. They made two contributions of the first importance. They wrote books, which were smuggled into England in surprisingly large numbers and showed the English people that their Government was not necessarily right in all it said about the Catholic religion. And they founded the Colleges at Douay, Rome and elsewhere, from which a stream of well-trained and ardent priests came into the country from 1574 onward. Without these priests, the great Catholic rally of Elizabeth's middle years could never have taken place.

Among the first converts of the missionary priests was Margaret Clitherow, for she was reconciled to the Church in 1574, the year of their arrival. And she was typical of the kind of convert they mostly made. For she belonged to the generation—then in its twenties—which had childhood memories of an all-Catholic England. Some say that as many as fifty thousand, the cream of the country's young manhood and young womanhood, thus swung back to the Church. The swing became even stronger after the first Jesuit mission of 1580-81.

This great youth movement filled the Government with alarm, for it was capturing the very people on whom its own success depended. Hence, the third ten years of Elizabeth's reign are filled with a savage endeavor to quell this movement among the young. A string of laws was passed, mounting in ferocity and culminating in the terrible statute of 1585 called "27 Elizabeth." And here, too, Margaret Clitherow was in the van. Though her case holds special features, hers was one of the earliest arrests under this statute.

Margaret Clitherow died in 1586. Two years later came the Armada, cutting Elizabeth's reign in two. To those who lived after, the first thirty years of her reign soon became unintelligible, if only because those who remembered Catholic England were dying out. Even today, when we talk about the Elizabethan Age, the pictures in our minds are generally taken from the years after the Armada. For instance, it was after the Armada, and in spite of the proved loyalty of Catholics, that the Government used against them the two weapons which really defeated them—fines on a scale that beggared all but the wealthiest families, and a fully developed system of espionage. These were only beginning on a small scale in the lifetime of Margaret Clitherow. It is vital to remember that she belongs to those forgotten thirty years in which the English people laboriously awoke to the truth that, if they wanted to keep their Faith, they must be ready to pay a heavy price in suffering.

While many things contributed to that awakening, the last stab was given by a single incident—the execution of Thomas Percy, Earl of Northumberland, the beloved leader of the Rising in the North. He had escaped into Scotland but was handed back to his own government. In 1572, after two years in prison, his head was cut off. If the Government had executed him as a political offender, it would have been within its rights. It put itself in the wrong by offering him his life if he would abjure his religion. He refused, and that refusal, more than anything, crystallized the new attitude of the English Catholics.

ST. MARGARET CLITHEROW

"Be thou faithful until death: and I will give thee the crown of life."

—Apocalypse 2:10

⌒ Chapter I ⌒
Growing Up

IN the year 1530, a certain Thomas Middleton took up his freedom as a citizen of York. It is possible that he came of a family of country gentlemen, for younger sons of such families in those days often took to trade. What is certain is that he went into business as a wax-chandler and that his wife's name was Jane. Their house was in the street called the Davygate, and there their four children were born—two boys, Thomas and Robert, and two girls, Alice and Margaret. We do not know the order of their births, but as Margaret was probably born about 1553 it looks as if she was one of the younger children.

All we know of her childhood is that she was brought up a Protestant and that she was not taught to read. This last does not mean that she was a neglected child; it only means that the closing down of the religious orders had involved the confiscation of nearly the whole educational endowment of the country. When Margaret was a little girl of ten, the Speaker of the House of Commons had some forcible things to say about the growing ignorance of the people. In other ways, however, she was well taught. She received a first-class training in housewifery, which in those days meant far more than it does now. A girl had to master a dozen different crafts, such as baking bread and brewing ale, and also she had to learn to supervise the weavers, tailors and others who came to the house to work. In addition, a woman of the citizen class was expected to be able to run her husband's business while he was away. In all these things Margaret, we are told, excelled. She worked hard herself, and expected hard work from others.

When Mary Tudor died and her sister Elizabeth came to the throne, Margaret was probably about five years old, hardly old enough to take in what was happening with any clearness. A law was passed forbidding the Mass and ordering the whole population to attend the new services in English in the parish churches. Very few people at all understood what was happening. A large number of the clergy conformed, especially in the country districts, and this helped to confuse the people still more. In the towns, however, where the clergy were better educated and quicker-minded men, a certain number stood out against the new laws. One of these was the Middletons' parish priest, Father Henry More. He must have refused with some spirit, for he was not only deprived of his living, but his private property was sequestered as well, so that he was reduced to poverty.

In spite of this good example, the Middletons conformed to the new laws. As a family they remained Protestant, though one or two of them subsequently returned to the Church. They accepted the Elizabethan Settlement, not only about church-going, but about regarding the Queen as the Supreme Head of the Church in England. That is what being a Protestant meant at the beginning of Elizabeth's reign—that the Mass was wrong and that the Queen was the Head of the Church. Those who conformed could count on favor and prosperity. The Government's plan was to restrict public office to those who would publicly profess their adherence to the Queen's supremacy in religion. At first, there were so few Protestants in the country that it was impossible to find recruits for an all-Protestant official class. Hence, for some years a good many Catholics still acted as justices of the peace and as sheriffs, and this helped to confuse people's minds still further. They simply could not take in that the Government seriously meant to destroy the Faith altogether.

Thomas Middleton conformed and prospered. He was a member of the Common Council of York, and in 1564, when Margaret was eleven, he was made one of the two sheriffs of the city. It was not quite such an occasion for rejoicing as one would expect, for the new sheriff was so ill with gout that a deputation had to be sent from the Council to receive his oath in his own house. Later in the year, he was so ill that he had to be excused his duties altogether, and for the last three years of his life he seems to have been a thoroughly sick man. In 1567, when Margaret was fourteen, Thomas Middleton died. When his will was read, it was found that he had left money to the poor of York to pray for the repose of his soul. So hard did even professing Protestants find it to believe that all their old landmarks were to be swept away.

Four months after her father's death, something happened which may not have startled Margaret as much as it does us: her mother married again. This would not have shocked Elizabethan opinion as badly as it does ours, though, even so, it was a short widowhood. What scandalized Jane Middleton's friends was that her choice fell on a man without wealth or standing, who owed his entry into the inner circle of York citizens entirely to his marriage with her. With a managing wife behind him, however, Henry Maye did very well. He became Alderman and at last Lord Mayor of York. And then his luck deserted him. Just before he became mayor his wife died. And before the year of his office was out, his stepdaughter Margaret had been put to death for her religion. Afterwards, all we hear of him is that he got into financial difficulties and had to ask for time to pay his debts. Without a wife at his back, he does not seem to have been very well able to stand on his own feet.

Father Mush is distinctly acid about Mr. Henry Maye, and one may hazard the guess that he was the kind of man whom women like, while men cannot stand. Jane Middleton clearly liked him. Even more important, Margaret liked him too—

and she had four years in which to study him through the intolerant eyes of adolescence, for he came to live in their house in the Davygate. There are two reasons for thinking she was fond of her stepfather. He was allowed to visit her in prison before her execution, which looks as if he were known to have influence with her. And when her first baby was born, she named him Henry. There seems no near relation after whom the child could have been called save her stepfather, Mr. Henry Maye. Where Father Mush is severe, Margaret seems to have had a soft spot.

Sheriff Middleton's death comes almost at the end of those first ten years of Elizabeth's reign, during which the country apparently accepted the change of religion with nothing worse than a grumble or two. The next seven years, when Margaret was growing up from fourteen to twenty-one, cover that pitiful phase when the country tried political and military action to recover the Faith and found that the Government was too strong to be shaken that way. These were the years of the flight of Mary Queen of Scots into England, of the Rising in the North and its harsh suppression, and of the Papal excommunication of Elizabeth. Two years later came the beheading of Blessed Thomas Percy, Earl of Northumberland, which, as we said, marks a turning-point in the attitude of English Catholics. At last they began to understand that nothing but martyrdom would save the country for the Faith.

In 1571, the year between the Queen's excom-

munication and the martyrdom of Blessed
Thomas Percy, Margaret Middleton married. We
think of her as eighteen, a beautiful girl with a
mass of light brown hair and a clear skin—no one
seems to have mentioned the color of her eyes.
But her greatest charm was her vivacity, an
unquenchable gaiety which hid, perhaps even
from herself, the deeps in her character. As she
also had a good dowry and a first-rate training in
housewifery, these varied attractions entitled her
to make a good match.

And so she did, in a worldly point of view—her
mother Jane Maye probably saw to that. For at
first sight the man she married does not seem the
most likely choice for a lively girl. He was a wid-
ower, John Clitherow, by trade a butcher, the one
Protestant among three brothers, and one of the
wealthiest citizens of York. We know that he was
rich because he was assessed for poor relief at the
highest rate for any save the aldermen themselves. In taking a wife from a Protestant family,
he may have meant to mark that he had broken
with the Catholic side. After the Rising, only two
years before his marriage, there had been heads
on pikes over Micklegate Bar, and perhaps to
John Clitherow they spoke eloquently of the wisdom of "putting himself wholly to her Highness's
[Elizabeth's] mercy, abjuring the Pope, and con-
forming himself to the new alteration [of reli-
gion]."[1] That they could speak a different message

---

1. From the document called *A Device for the Alteration of
   Religion,* in which someone, probably Cecil himself, drew

to the bride at his side probably never entered his head. She seemed born for unthinking enjoyment of the good things of this world, and for that very reason a "safe" choice in those perilous times.

If such were John Clitherow's hopes, he was doomed to disappointment. Within three years, his wife had become a Catholic. We know nothing of the steps by which she came to this decision, though we can make one or two guesses in the light of known facts. After all, both her husband's brothers were Catholics, and one of them became a priest. Beyond this, we know something of the considerations which weighed with her generation. This is one of the points where we have to remind ourselves that Margaret Clitherow belongs to the first thirty years of Elizabeth's reign, when all but the youngest could still remember an all-Catholic England. Once the Faith ceased to be a matter of living memory, converts began to tell stories as elaborate as they do today. And they often needed a trip abroad to start them thinking. But in Margaret's lifetime, young people just grown up did not need to travel in order to find the footprints of the Church, and their own memory could correct impressions derived from sermons. Hence, where a seventeenth-century convert, Sir Toby Matthew, could list twenty-four separate reasons for becoming a Catholic, Margaret's generation could be content

---

up the policy whereby the English nation was to be deprived of its ancestral religion.

with two. The considerations that counted for most at the beginning of Elizabeth's reign were the consolation of Catholic worship and the ancientry of the Catholic religion. Margaret spoke for her whole generation when in prison she made her profession of faith:

"I am," she said, "fully resolved in all things touching my Faith, which I ground upon Jesu Christ, and by Him I steadfastly believe to be saved: which Faith I acknowledge to be the same that He left to His Apostles, and they to their successors from time to time, and is taught in the Catholic Church through all Christendom, and promised to remain with her unto the world's end, and hell-gates shall not prevail against it; and by God's assistance I mean to live and die in the same Faith; for if an angel come from heaven, and preach any other doctrine than we have received, the Apostle biddeth us not believe him."

≈ Chapter II ≈
Husband and Wife:
Diverging Paths

WHEN Margaret Clitherow married, she left the house in the Davygate where she had been born and went to live in her husband's house in the butchers' quarter of York; for in those days men practicing the same trade lived in the same part of the town. The most likely tradition says that her new home was the house now known as No. 36, The Shambles. Another favors No. 3, the Little Shambles. These streets have changed as little as any in the ancient city of York. The houses are still the over-hanging, wooden-fronted dwellings which Margaret knew. On the ground floor were the shops. Behind and above, the families lived, so that the wife could keep an eye on her husband's business when he was away. In the case of a butcher's wife, this was specially necessary, as the butcher might have to be away for days at a time buying cattle for slaughter.

John Clitherow was not a bad sort of man, but he had no idea of bringing unpleasantness on himself for the sake of his religion. He seems to have ended his days as a Protestant. But at first he was what Catholics called a "schismatic" and Protestants a "church Papist." That means that he went to the English services in his parish church at the Government's bidding, but secretly preferred the Catholic religion. Church Papists offered many excuses for this behavior. The services, they pointed out, were unobjectionable; and as for the sermon, there was no need to listen to that. Some even went so far as to receive Communion according to the Protestant rite, on the grounds that, since it was no true Sacrament, it was a meaningless act and so harmless. Even the decision of the Church, taken at the Council of Trent, forbidding them to purchase safety by deceit, often did not alter their conduct.

Bad as that conduct was, they were in a most painful position. An open Catholic, that is, one who refused to go to the parish church, had to pay a fine of a shilling for every absence, which is more like fifteen shillings today. If he persisted, he could be imprisoned. Besides official penalties, he had to suffer much unofficial robbery. All public office was closed to him, and if he were in business, he risked ruin; either he lost business, or else customers could refuse to pay for work done, and the law would give him no redress. To a man with his living to get, open profession of Catholicism meant bringing his children to want. Only the wealthy landed families could hold out—and as we saw, they were at a later state attacked by enormous fines. Concern for their children did more to drive the men of England from the Faith than torture, imprisonment and death.

As a result, in a good many families the husband conformed while his wife did not. He paid her fines, let her bring up the children as Catholics, and was careful not to know if Mass were said in his house. One reason for the very slow death of the Faith in England was that the mother again and again passed it on to her children, while the father waited for his deathbed to be reconciled to the Church. But inevitably, men who acted like this tended to drift insensibly into real heresy. After all, every sermon they heard contained some attack on the Church. If people hear a thing often enough, without ever meeting a reply that grips their attention, they generally end by believing it. This is the principle of all propaganda and all advertising. The Government judged very shrewdly when it insisted that every single person must come within earshot of its licensed preachers once a week.

John Clitherow, however, went further than simply going to church. He was prepared to accept public office, which means that he was prepared to declare publicly that he accepted the Queen's supremacy in religion. Six months before he married Margaret, he had been made a bridgemaster, that is, one of the citizens responsible for the upkeep of the bridge over the Ouse. Now, on the Ousebridge was one of the worst prisons in York, the one where Margaret was to spend her last days on earth. And close to it was the building called the Toll Booth, where she was to die. There is something ironic in the position; in the months when John Clitherow was preparing to bring home his bride, he was also, all unwittingly, helping to prepare the place of her death. If he could have looked ahead those fifteen years, would he, one wonders, have chosen as he did?

In 1572, the year after his marriage, John Clitherow was one of the men specially sworn in, in every parish, to keep a look out for "the late rebels and other evil-disposed persons suspected of Papistry." This was a small matter—indeed, it is possible that he could have salved his conscience by saying that if this business could be kept in the hands of local men, they would be able to protect their Papist neighbors; for the citizens of York were very, very unwilling to put the law into force against the Catholics. More than in any other part of the country, the Government had to send special emissaries to the North to carry out its policy.

The year 1574, however, brought crisis to both husband and wife. She became a Catholic, he a chamberlain. This was an important piece of promotion, for a chamberlain of York was entitled to be addressed as "Mr." and took rank as a gentleman; all social distinctions were much more sharply defined then than now. And so, at the very time of her reconciliation to the Church, Margaret Clitherow had to see her husband take this decisive step into bondage to the powers of this world. For the more he owed to the world, the harder would it become to break the net in which it held him. And every such promotion meant a fresh affirmation of his acceptance of the royal supremacy in religion.

To make it yet harder for her to bear, both his brothers were making a firm stand. Of one, a draper, we know little save that he was a staunch Catholic. But the other brother, William, must have touched Margaret's life in some profoundly personal way, for she named a child after him. The baby born in the year of her reconciliation was a little girl, Anne—and the only Anne in Margaret's story was a Mrs. Anne Tesh, a noted Catholic, who for some days shared Margaret's prison cell, and who clearly was a close friend. Quite possibly it was after her that little Anne Clitherow was named.

But two years later we get another clue. In 1576, a list of recusants* mentions that Margaret was in prison, and pregnant. Now, 1576 was in all probability the year in which her brother-in-law, William Clitherow, entered the College at Douay to study for the priesthood, for we hear of his ordination six years later. Did Margaret and her brother-in-law talk out together their difficulties? It is even possible that it was her gay, gallant example which set him thinking of consecrating his life to the service of God. The dates, at any rate, suggest that baby William's name is a memorial of precious sympathy and help within her family circle.

---

*See note on p. xi.—*Publisher*, 2003.

Not that John Clitherow was exactly hostile. Like many others he probably expected the Faith to return before very long, and he did not wish to be too completely on the wrong side of the fence when that should happen. So he made things as easy as he could for his wife. He turned his broad back and was careful to know nothing of the priests who came to his house to say Mass. Nor did he stint her of money, which one satirist hints was the usual fate of a church Papist's wife. Margaret always had money for her works of charity. Her life in prison had shown her how poor prisoners might literally starve to death if no one came to their aid. Her alms to prisoners and their families were constant and abundant and, to do John Clitherow justice, he never seems to have complained.

They had their tiffs. Margaret admits to "such small matters as are commonly incident to husband and wife," and one may suspect that her own temper was on the quick side. One of the things they differed about was the shop. John Clitherow was a wholesale butcher and not merely a retailer, and since the wholesale business brought them in a very good income, Margaret wished to give up the shop; she did not like too great eagerness to make money. Indeed, she knew very well that this was the weak point in her husband's character. Perhaps she hoped that if he would conquer his desire for gain at this point, it might start him on the road of his conversion. But he would not listen to her—she was in fact thoroughly out of fashion in being so free from the get-rich-quick mania which was seizing the country. In the end, she had to content herself with another outlet for her feeling about money, in some ways smaller and yet of great importance; before they began selling in the mornings, she used to send out to learn what other butchers were charging and charge the same. She would not attract business by underselling nor make an unfair profit by overcharging. In an age of hustle and grab, Margaret loved her neighbor as herself, whether he came to her as a customer or a rival tradesman.

Her husband's personal kindness, however, did not at all lessen for Margaret the conflict of loyalties in which she was caught. These conflicts of loyalties are among the most painful trials to which human beings can be subjected. St. Thomas More named one when, on the scaffold, he said: "I die the King's good servant, but God's first." Every martyr of the sixteenth and seventeenth centuries could have echoed him, for their main conflict lay between the claims of God and of the Government. In the case of Margaret Clitherow, there was something further. Where St. Thomas More was the head of his family, Margaret was under the authority of her husband. She thus had to take into account her duty towards two earthly authorities, not only the civil government, but her husband as well. And naturally, it was the domestic conflict which was the more painful. Where More protested his loyalty to the King, Margaret protested her love for her husband. "Know you," she declared, "that I love him next unto God in this world. . . . If I have offended my husband in anything, but for my conscience [i.e., but for my religious duty], I ask God and him forgiveness."

That he obligingly turned his back for her convenience did not really comfort her. Part of her grief sprang from the fact that, to him, it should be *only* a question of convenience, not of principle. Besides, her frank, open nature found concealment abhorrent. What nerved her to hide things from him was the knowledge that her duty to God involved her husband in personal danger, if it became known that she had Mass said in his house. But she hated the need to keep him in the dark, and it was an abiding misery to her that he should be so blind to his highest good. Behind all her gaiety, she lived with a sword in her heart.

Because she felt all this so keenly, she tried to make it up to him by being, in all save her conscience, just as good a wife as she could be. Here she succeeded. John Clitherow was in the habit of saying that he could wish for no better wife, "except only for two faults, as he thought, and those were, because she fasted too much, and would not go with him to church." Since conscience forced her to go against him in matters of moment, the same conscience obliged her to see that he should have no cause of complaint over anything else.

As time went on, things grew harder, not easier, for as more severe laws were passed, the trouble she might bring on her husband grew graver. When the worst of the Penal Acts was passed, the terrible statute of 1585, under which most of the martyrs suffered, a timid Catholic came and remonstrated with her. His advice was "to be more careful of herself, and since that virtue and the Catholic cause was now made treason and felony [i.e., since it was now treason to be a priest and felony to harbor one], that either she would not with such danger receive any priest at all, or else very seldom: and this added also, that it was no wisdom to admit her children and others to God's service [i.e., to Mass in her house], and that she ought not to venture upon these things without license of her husband."

This talk left Margaret worried, though her good sense told her that nothing ought to be allowed to come before obedience to God. It was three days before she had a chance to consult Father Mush. "May I not," she asked him, "receive priests and serve God as I have done, notwithstanding these new laws, without my husband's consent? . . . I know not how the rigor of these new statutes may alter my duty in this thing: but if you tell me that I offend God in any point, I will not do it for all the world."

Father Mush put three points to her in his reply. First, it was for her husband's own safety that he should know as little as possible about Mass being said in his house. Second, that no laws of man could alter her duty to God, no matter how cruel they might be; and that where her duty to

God was concerned, she was not under the authority of her husband, but directly answerable to her own conscience. Thirdly, that anyone obeying these wicked laws shared in the guilt of those who enacted them.

This last was a point likely to come home to Margaret with great force, for she had an extraordinarily sensitive conscience about leading others into sin, or making worse what they were already doing wrong. She carried this to such lengths that she refused to allow a friend to bribe her executioners to finish her off quickly, for fear of increasing their guilt. Her judges, jury and executioners were to be the object of her solicitous charity, a charity so rare that no one was able to guess what was in her mind until she told them.

Yet it was no sudden spurt of noble sentiment that carried Margaret through her martyrdom. It was the habits she had been steadily practicing, at home or in prison, for twelve years, above all the habit of putting God first in all her actions. Then there was a further habit of looking carefully to see how what she was doing would help or hinder others in pleasing God. At the end, we see her standing on a shining pinnacle of consummate charity. But she had climbed there, step by step, through the day-to-day relations with her husband, children and servants. The high charity of her death was all of a piece with her life.

∽ Chapter III ∽

Mother and Home

MARGARET Clitherow was in some sort a martyr of motherhood. That is to say, the special poignancy of her martyrdom lies in her perfect surrender of these dearest earthly ties. For her, they were exceptionally strong ties. For Margaret was a woman of strong affections, whose home was a center of absorbing interest, an outlet for all her great vitality of mind and body. Left to herself, she would have poured all her devotedness into her relations with her husband and children.

Her religion thus came to her in part as a corrective of that danger of selfishness which lies in all human love. But it also brought a strong intensification of that love. Margaret loved her children more because she loved God most. And she loved them more wisely. She learned to stand back a little, looking beyond their passing enjoyments to the enduring happiness which can only spring from good habits and a stable character. Above all, she learned to look beyond their happiness on earth to their bliss in Heaven. Her love became both more intimate and more detached.

From an early age, she began to teach her children such little lessons in self-sacrifice as they were able to learn, which yet made them happier children than if they had always gotten their own way.

The spirit of Margaret's motherhood comes out in a casual phrase which she used to one of the Protestant preachers sent to harass her in prison. A fairly common saying about a woman martyr is that "she went to her death as to a bridal." Father Mush said that about Margaret, and once she said it about herself. But as her death drew very near, she used another expression, so unexpected that at first it is almost a shock, even though we know that in those days people spoke frankly of much that we now by-pass in talk. She said: "I confess death is fearful and flesh is frail, yet I mind [intend] by God's assistance to spend my blood in this Faith as willingly as ever I put my paps into my children's mouths." It shows what Margaret felt about her motherhood that she should speak of it thus simply in the same breath with her martyrdom.

Now comes another remarkable point. Not one of Margaret's children was under her care after the age of twelve. Henry was fourteen when she died, but had been sent abroad to school two years earlier. Anne was twelve, and William perhaps nine or ten at the time of her death. Nor had Margaret had them in her care even for the whole of those short years; she had been separated from them by her imprisonments, once for two years on end. And after her death, efforts were made to turn William and Anne against their mother's religion. Yet it was all in vain. Margaret remained for their whole lives the strongest influence over her children. They remained true to her teaching all their days, Henry and William becoming priests and Anne a nun. This hold on her children was one of Margaret's outstanding feats.

Yet it was not achieved by any softness. Margaret won her children's hearts and had their confidence, but not by indulging them. Indeed, we today might consider her unduly strict. At that time, English methods of upbringing rather shocked the people of other countries by their severity, and Margaret seems to have followed the ideas of her age and country. At least, we find her speaking of "children, which with an apple and a rod you may make to say what you will." It was not true of her own children, who showed remarkable staunchness under threats, some say under whipping as well; whatever line she took, Margaret did not break their spirit. But she did bring them up hardily, with a strong sense of duty. And this was taught, as it is best taught to children, through the little duties of their day.

Any strictness in their training, however, was offset for the children by the glad, free atmosphere of their home. There was nothing morose or bleak about Margaret. Father Mush devotes a whole chapter to *Her Alacrity and Joy in Mind and Body*. "All her actions," he tells us, "were tempered with all inward tranquility, and with discreet and honest mirth, with mild smiling countenance: ready of tongue, but yet her words modest, and courteous, and lowly; quick in the despatch of business, and then most pleasant when she could most serve God [go to Mass] and procure the same for others. . . . Thus in all her actions she served God with joy and gladness, without fretting or lumpish mind."

What a delightful mother to be brought up by! One feels sure that Margaret did not keep her charming manners for visitors and forget to be courteous to her children. For children are very sensitive to good manners, that real considerateness which is quick to read feelings, with a knack of saying the right thing at the right moment, all bathed in laughter and high spirits. Neither their daily round nor their religion was allowed to become dispiriting to them. Everything was shot through with love and laughter.

As for their religion, it met them not as a duty but as a privilege. What fortunate children they were, to have Our Blessed Lord Himself so often in their own home! And if they had to pay for this sometimes by having to go without their mother, because she had been haled off to prison, it taught them to turn for help direct to Our Lord and His Holy Mother. So they too learned to put God before what was dearest to them on earth, their lovely, smiling mother, who made even hard things seem delightfully well worth doing. And she, on her side, was exercised again and again in her more difficult renunciation, putting God before her darling Henry and Anne. It rather looks as if once she may have come home from prison with baby William in her arms, though it is possible that she was allowed to go home for the birth. Margaret gave her children to God, not in words, but in painful deeds. But because she gave them to Him, God could hold them for her in her absences, yes, in the long absence of her death; so that by loving God first, the family was held together as it could not otherwise have been.

To Margaret, forced to shut her husband out from the joy at the core of her life, it must have been the deepest comfort to bring her children in. Her house was one of the chief Mass centers of York, and her children were admitted to all that was afoot. It was natural that they should know how their tutor could slip out of the window of their attic schoolroom and escape through the house next door. But they knew much more than that. They knew the secret of the cupboard where the vestments were kept, and the altar breads (which they called by the charming old English name of singing breads or singing cakes). They knew, too, the priest's hole in their own house and another at a distance. For when her house was too closely watched for Mass to be safely said there, Margaret rented a room some distance off and there, too, provided a hiding place. Tradition says this was in the Black Swan Inn at Pease-holme Green, which is likely enough, for innkeepers were among those who clung longest to the old Faith; that is one reason why the missionary priests could move about the country with a measure of security. The entry to this other priest's hole, however, was somewhat awkward. One of the duties of Margaret's boys seems to have been to show the Father how to wriggle himself in!

The mention of the tutor and schoolroom brings us to another striking point. Margaret was so intelligent herself that she may well have felt keenly her own lack of education and have determined to give her children a better start. But even that did not content her; she wanted to learn herself. During one of her imprisonments, she learned to read English, both print and handwriting. The tutor she gave to her children was a Catholic, though this was against the law. Only a Protestant might act as teacher to children. And it was not enough for him to profess adherence to the Queen's supremacy in religion; he had to have a license from the bishop, and before the license was granted there was a searching examination into the doctrines he held.

Still, this difficulty was in a sense a simplification. So few men in the North could satisfy the bishops that there were few schools. Therefore, it did not look odd for Margaret to keep her children home from school, for there was nowhere to send them. So she did not attract universal attention by quietly giving them a tutor at home, a Mr. Stapleton, whom she employed to teach not only her own children, but those of some Catholic neighbors.

This undoubtedly increased the danger. No one, however, seems to have worried much about the children, though in fact it was from one of the little outsiders that danger was to come. Most people would have said that the point of risk was the tutor himself. The Government was beginning to use against its own subjects the terrible weapon of espionage, and though the spy system was not yet fully organized, the authorities were on the look-out for disgruntled employees who could be frightened or bribed or even tortured into betraying their employers. A case in which a tutor was involved led to an execution a few months before Margaret's own. It did not stand alone, and Catholics were growing uneasy as they realized that any member of their household might be induced to inform against them.

Mr. Stapleton seems to have commanded confidence. When Father Mush grew anxious about how things were going in that house, it was neither the children nor the tutor that he remarked on; it was the servants. Margaret was no slacker herself, nor did she easily tolerate slackness in others. One day Father Mush asked her "how she durst be so sharp with her servants when they offended by slacking their duties, since they might procure to her much danger if they revealed, upon any displeasure or grief [grievance], the priest's being there." Margaret's servants were deeply attached to their mistress, and indeed she was an unusual mistress—she liked to keep the roughest work in the house for herself. And her reason for letting her "maidens" do some of it was equally unusual: she felt it would be selfish to keep such an opportunity for humility to herself. Her maids knew well that she asked nothing of them which she would be unwilling to set her own hands to, and Margaret was justified in trusting to their loyalty. Yet this is not the reason she gave to Father Mush. That is as unexpected as all the rest. "God defend [forbid]" she replied to his remonstrance, "that for my Christian liberty in serving Him [for the sake of having Mass in her house] I should neglect my duty to my servants, or not correct them as they deserve. God shall dispose all as it pleaseth Him: but I will not be blamed for their faults, nor fear any danger for this good cause." This is a further example of the thing we noted before, Margaret's sensitive horror of leading others into sin.

As this chapter is mainly about Margaret's children, let us finish it with a short account of the one of whom we know most, Anne. When Margaret was arrested, her husband and children were arrested too and confined separately. Anne was placed "in ward," which seems to mean in the charge of Protestants, by whom she was "used extremely," that is, treated with great harshness to make her go to church. Exactly what this harsh usage was is not certain, but whatever it was, Anne stood up pluckily to it. And then a singularly heartless trick was played upon her.

After Margaret was dead, Anne was told that she would save her mother's life if she would go to church and hear a sermon. Then she yielded— once. But when she realized the cruel deceit that had been practiced on her, she returned to her refusal and never again gave in.

Shortly after Margaret's death, John Clitherow was allowed to take his children home. But Anne did not settle down. When she was fourteen, she tried to run away from home, was caught, and this time jailed in good earnest, not in York, but at Lancaster. And in prison she remained until she was eighteen. Her father then married again, a Protestant, of course, and got the Lord Mayor of York to write to the authorities asking that his daughter be allowed to come home, promising too that learned divines should confer with her and convince her of the truth of the Protestant religion. On these representations, Anne was released. But the conferences proved useless; nothing could shake her faith and her constancy. After about three years, she slipped out of the country and entered the convent of the Austin [Augustinian] Canonesses in Louvain. The escape from England was not particularly difficult for a girl who had an uncle a priest and two brothers studying for the priesthood. Indeed, so many English girls entered convents in the Low Countries at this time that there must have been regular, though secret, arrangements for their travel.

At St. Ursula's in Louvain Anne found in authority that holy woman Mother Margaret

Clement, link with the great martyr of an earlier generation, St. Thomas More.[1] And among her companions were the sisters of martyr priests, and sometimes a widow ending her days in prayer. One of these widows may have had a specially poignant interest for Sister Anne Clitherow, for Widow Wiseman had been sentenced to the same death as Margaret Clitherow but reprieved by the Queen herself. In course of time, so many English nuns came to St. Ursula's that the Austin Canonesses decided to follow the example of the Benedictines and open a convent entirely for Englishwomen. The new convent was called St. Monica's, and most of the English nuns at St. Ursula's went there to make the foundation— even the aged Mother Margaret Clement. They had, however, to make a rule that no one might go to the new convent unless she had either a dowry or a maintenance from her friends. This cut out four English nuns, who had to remain at St. Ursula's; and one of the four was Sister Anne Clitherow. She was, however, a keen supporter of the new foundation, and her excellent business

---

1. The link is through that engaging little person, Margaret Giggs, whom St. Thomas More educated with his own children. It was she who dressed up as a milkmaid to succor the Carthusians being starved to death in the Tower. She married Dr. Clement, the tutor More had given to his children, and had eleven children, to all of whom she taught Latin and Greek. Mother Margaret Clement was the youngest of the eleven. She become an Austin Canoness and was Superior at St. Ursula's when Anne Clitherow entered.

sense was of great service to the new Superior—
Anne seems to have inherited her father's business head and her mother's generosity. She also
had her mother's desire for education; the first
thing she did in her convent was to learn Latin
"almost entirely by her own efforts, so that she
understood it perfectly." And she used to teach
Latin to the English postulants who were sent
from St. Monica's to the Motherhouse to absorb
the traditions of their order.

Margaret's only legacy to Anne had been her
shoes and stockings. The little girl took the hint.
"Sister Anne Clitherow," say her convent annals,
"followed well her holy mother's virtuous foot-
steps, for she was a very good religious, and one
that set herself very seriously to the way of perfection."[2] Yes. One can understand that Anne
Clitherow was rather a serious character. The second persecuted generation was much less merry
than the first. Margaret could pass on her faith,
courage and constancy, but not her sparkling gaiety. Part of her martyrdom, surely, was to know
that for her children the lights of this world might
well be quenched.

---

2. Quoted from *A Link Between Flemish Mystics and English
   Martyrs* by C. S. Durrant, p. 229. From this book the
   details here given about Anne Clitherow have mainly been
   taken.

∽ Chapter IV ∽

"This Golden Woman"

HAD Margaret Clitherow any faults? Father Mush asked himself this question. He admitted that she had some imperfections—I myself feel sure she had a fairly quick temper. But after thinking hard, the only thing he could call a real fault was a slight failure in prudence: he felt it not entirely well-judged to let her children know everything about how Mass was said in their house. And even there he admitted that there were excuses.

We have to remember that Father Mush knew Margaret only in her last years, when her character had reached what was to prove its final phase of holiness. We have to read between the lines to find out what sort of person she was both before and after her conversion, in the years when her character was in process of formation.

That character was of an extremely positive kind. Clear-headed, strong-willed, warm-hearted, Margaret Clitherow could never have been "good" in a colorless way. Part of the charm of her holiness is that it was as colorful, varied and sparkling as her natural character, and as full of unexpected turns. It is an enchanting picture that Father Mush draws for us. Yet if we go behind the enchantment we get the impression that, at the start, she must have been about as self-willed and headstrong as a human being can well be.

Margaret's school of holiness, Father Mush tells us, was prison. It was this that gave her that leisure for God which is a necessity for those who are to learn His secrets. In prison, he explains, "the servants of God (as delivered from all worldly cares and business) might learn most commodiously every Christian virtue. . . . For every day, she, growing stronger than herself, marvelously increased in fervour and charity to God and man, planted in her heart a perfect contempt for this world, and laboured principally to overcome herself in all disordered passions and inclinations of nature, that her actions and service might be acceptable in the sight of God, as she preferred His honour and will before all things."

Few things more distressed Margaret than to hear of Catholics in prison who did not recognize their privileges. Succoring prisoners was her chief work of charity; for in those days prisoners had to pay for their own keep, and if they could not do so, they were left to starve to death. But though she never grew slack in caring for their needs, it was their spiritual privileges that most impressed her. "Though she exceeded in compassion, yet never saw I her heavy or sorrowful for the poverty, tribulation, or persecution which fell to any, so long as they showed their patience and gladness to suffer for God's sake; whereas, if she had seen any contrary disposition or behavior in them, she would have sighed and lamented, and earnestly prayed for them." It hurt her deeply to hear of Catholics in prison who, instead of drawing nearer to God, were preoccupied with making things more comfortable for themselves, indulging, says Father Mush, "in idleness, impatience, covetousness, murmuration, dissension or forwardness, self-love, or greedy desire of liberty, worldly pleasure or any other thing inconvenient [unfitting] to their calling, which should be mortified to the world and all the concupiscence thereof."

Margaret valued her time in prison as a chance for "getting of those virtues which I perceive to be wanting in me." It is characteristic that she should have thrown herself into gaining virtues rather than uprooting faults, for often the best way to weed out a fault is to cultivate the opposite virtue. It is also characteristic that she should have gone straight to the main point: the whole business resolved itself into one simple principle, to please God in all she did. This simplicity of motive lies at the heart of Margaret's holiness. It was the compass by which she steered her course through stormy seas, the touchstone whereby she tested her own actions and those of others, particularly those for whom she was in any way responsible. This was her "Little Way"—to refer all her actions to God. In the busy life she led at home it was not possible to keep God before her thoughts continuously; but she tried to carry out every action with the purpose of pleasing Him. When this purpose slipped from her mind, she blamed herself strongly: "Methinks I do nothing well, because I overslipped this right intention which God's servants should always have, actually, to do and refer all my doings to His glory." But she was the only person to think she did nothing well. Everyone else was amazed at her skill, her diligence, and the wisdom she brought to all her undertakings.

This longing for God made her look back regretfully to her life in prison, and the prisons of those days were dirty, smelly, vermin-ridden places where prisoners suffered from constant overcrowding and underfeeding. Under the new Penal Laws, it was the most respectable part of the nation which was crowded into them, to be tyrannized over by brutal jailers. In spite of Father Mush's rather severe remarks on the behavior of some, we have to place on record that the Catholic prisoners of those days normally practiced more fasting and more watching than circumstances forced on them. Apart from any other reason, they soon discovered by experience that, unless they ruled their bodily desires with a firm hand, they lacked the spiritual strength to face their ordeal. Most of them, however, had a natural wish to return to their ordinary life in the world. But upon Margaret, the effect of her prison life was to make her long to end her days in some convent, in order to give her whole attention to God. She had already learned to read English in prison. Now she learned to say the Matins of Our Lady in Latin, in order to be so far ready for convent life when she should be set free from her other duties.

At home, her constant round of domestic claims was not allowed to interfere with her life of prayer. If possible, she liked to begin the day with Mass. When this could not be done, since at times the house was too closely watched, she rose early to spend an hour or two in prayer. Learning to read had opened to her another source of help; among her treasures was a copy of the New Testament in English, newly smuggled in from Rheims, and also the *Imitation of Christ*. All the fasts of the Church were strictly kept; and on Fridays, if she could get leave from her "ghostly father," she took the discipline. For in all she did she was most careful to render strict obedience to her director. Father Mush particularly comments on this spirit of obedience. She wanted her life to be a Way of the Cross, and in this spirit she welcomed all the trouble stirred up for her by her persecutors. When they left her alone, she tried to let no day pass "without something voluntarily taken whereby she might suffer pain, either of mind or body." She longed to suffer for God, and felt it must be for some fault in her that He withheld the chance of suffering prison and death for His sake.

And she contrived to be a pilgrim. The great shrines of England were dishonored and defaced. But the Government, all unwitting, was making a new kind of shrine, the places of execution where the martyrs suffered. Outside York, at the great gallows of Knavesmire, the moldering remains of martyrs sometimes hung for many days. Knavesmire to Margaret was holy ground. With a party of friends, she would slip out of the city after dark to pray at the hallowed spot. She made these pilgrimages barefoot, and was so lost in prayer that she had to be dragged away at dawn when the light made it dangerous to be found there.

But the heart and center of her life was the Mass. The only thing that could dim her gaiety was to have no priest in her house. "This is a war and a trial in God's Church," she would say, "and, therefore, if I cannot do my duty without peril and dangers, yet by God's grace I will not be slacker for them. If God's priests dare venture themselves to my house, I will never refuse them." "Her most delight," says Father Mush, "was to kneel where she might continually behold the Blessed Sacrament, and usually she chose her place next [to] the door, behind all the rest, in the worst and most base seats." And he draws a moving picture of her when she received Holy Communion. This she liked to do twice a week, which by the ideas of those times was very often indeed. "In the time of her receiving the Blessed Sacrament of Christ, His Body, she ever coveted to have the lowest place, so far as she could do it without trouble and noisomeness to others [without making a nuisance of herself], for she would not seem to any to desire it. While she received, her lowly and gracious countenance was washed with sweet tears trickling from her eyes. Afterwards she would depart for half an hour into some close corner, where she might familiarly enjoy the delights of her God, Whom she had brought into the secret parlor of her heart, and all the day after she would be merry and smiling, yet most wary to keep her senses shut, lest she should by negligence or false security be robbed of her treasure."

Among all the details of her character which Father Mush gives, two alone can find mention here. She was a very popular person, loved by her neighbors and able to persuade them when nobody else could. The Catholics of York owed a good deal to the skill with which she talked over Protestants who were wondering uncomfortably if they ought to denounce her to the authorities. And yet, with all her popularity, Margaret suffered much from the criticisms of the good. Now, here is the really remarkable touch. Margaret actually preferred the company of these critics to that of people who always spoke her fair.

The other thing was her spirit of mirth. This must have been something quite out of the ordinary. Father Mush devotes a chapter to it, and it comes into nearly all his other chapters. Margaret was a mirthful being, happiness suffused her, she moved in an atmosphere of joy. One feels that in her natural character she was a pleasure-loving Elizabethan, to whom high spirits and practical joking were common ingredients of life. Margaret carried this happy temper into her religion, where it took on new colors, like a cloud irradiated by a hidden sun. Her whole story, right up to the last, moves in this atmosphere of high-spirited fun.

Looking for Margaret's faults, then, does not get us anywhere. Let us then alter the question and ask instead what were her failures. And here, something at once comes into view. There was in Margaret's life one very big failure indeed: she was never able to convert her husband. She charmed him with her delightful brand of holiness; and all he did was to turn his back and let her go on her way alone. In the end, she set before him the deepest and most persuasive appeal of Christianity: martyrdom. And he turned from it. The great challenge of her death seems not to have drawn him nearer to the truth, but to have driven him farther away.[1]

Most of us, at some time in our lives, have been present at one of those curious incidents, trifling in themselves, which yet give the whole company a kind of electric shock. For an instant, the hidden fires of human nature break through the tidy sur-

---

1. It is as well to remember that John Clitherow compares favorably with some other husbands of Catholic wives. Some kept their wives short of money, paying their fines but docking their dress allowance. A few even denounced their wives to the authorities! In one such case the wife won her husband by her bearing under this trial. It remains all the stranger that a man with the good qualities we feel in John Clitherow should have been impervious, as far as we can tell, to the truth his wife made so attractive for him.

face of our daily behavior. In the story of Margaret Clitherow there is an incident of this kind. It startled all who saw it. It startled Father Mush when he heard of it. It startled Margaret herself. And though she furnished an explanation which is true and sound as far as it goes, one cannot feel that it goes the whole way. We are left asking, "Now, I wonder what lay behind that?"

It happened one day when she and her husband were dining with neighbors, Margaret being the only Catholic at the table. By chance the talk turned on Catholics and the Catholic religion. And John Clitherow, growing "liberal among the pots," began to swear and hold forth something like this: "I cannot tell," said he, "what Catholics are. They will fast, pray, give alms and punish themselves more than we all, yet they are of as evil disposition in other things as we." A tradesman ought to have known better, for it was a common saying that if a man paid his debts, he must be a Catholic. John Clitherow, however, went on to make ugly accusations against the personal morals of Catholics—with his wife sitting by, whose beauty had naturally made a certain amount of talk when she received priests in her house without her husband's knowledge. It is a tribute to Margaret that her nearest neighbors, Protestants among them, were those who most vigorously disbelieved these slanders. And one cannot help feeling that her husband had no idea that anyone could dream of applying these random words to his wife. Indeed, Margaret's great support amid all this unpleasant gossip had been the certainty that her husband trusted her absolutely. To have him hold forth like this must have been a cruel blow. At least, that was people's first idea, when suddenly and unaccountably, she burst into tears. And once begun, she could not stop.

John Clitherow, sobered by the unusual sight of his wife's tears, called her a fool and said he did not mean her—he could wish for no better wife. Other people told her he had only been joking and she must take it all in fun. It was no good. She cried and cried. Even when she recovered, she remained depressed for the rest of the day—she who was generally a center of laughter—and she passed a disturbed night. Not till next day did she see Father Mush, who had heard the story and, like everyone else, could not account for her breakdown. "Truly, Father," Margaret told him, "I was not then, nor am I now, anything at all sorry in respect of myself, for I thank God I have ever been a true and chaste wife to my husband, both in thought and deed; God and mine own conscience doth witness it; but it grieveth mine heart that he should so heinously offend God by slandering Catholics and the Catholic Church, whereby I fear me he shall more hardly come to God's grace and be a member of His Church. This thing only caused me to weep, and maketh me sorry still when I think on it."

This explanation will bear thinking over. For one thing, it shows how intensely Margaret had set her heart on her husband's conversion. This was natural, indeed, praiseworthy. But, is there not still a trace of selfishness in it? It shows how high she had climbed that we should even raise the point; but it does look as if she longed, not merely for his conversion, but for his conversion *by her means*. The temptation of her kind of character is that its mixture of strong affection and strong will may lead to tyranny, a demand that those she loves shall always be influenced by her, dependent on her, conditioned by her, not only in all they do, but also in all they think and feel. Margaret had been lifted by her religion above the coarser and commoner forms of this tyranny; in her it would take a spiritual form. Love for God had cleansed and steadied much that might have been selfish and unbalanced in her human love. And yet, it is possible that deep in her heart, Margaret cherished the hope that it would be *her* goodness and charm, *her* fasting and prayer, *her* constancy and example, *her* perfect discharge of her duties as wife and mother which should at last bring her husband to the fold of Christ. If this were so, it would be a last unsubdued stronghold of self-love in her heart. She was not ready for all God was going to ask of her until this last piece of self-assertion was cleansed away.

At the same time, there is another side. In this incident we see in a lightning flash something much bigger than the tragedy of one husband and one wife; we see the grand hope and disappointment of all her generation. Those young people who had turned from political action to spiritual action would hardly have been human if they had not expected that their spiritual campaign was going to succeed—that the constancy of martyrs and confessors would in fact win England for the Faith. But it did not. And as the realization of failure stole upon them, what an agony of disappointment they must have endured. All that heroic charity gone to waste! That is what it must have felt like. That is the surrender to God's will to which they had to attain. And when the surrender involved some dearly loved individual, it became about the hardest submission God can ever ask.

We here come up against the most frightening mystery of our religion, the mystery of grace and free will. God will persuade, solicit, plead; but He will not force the choice of any intelligent creature. His persuasion, solicitude, pleading was set before Elizabeth's England by His martyrs and confessors. It made a great stir, as popular ballads show. But in the main, it was rejected. And those martyrs and confessors, so delightfully human in their young eagerness, must have found it bewilderingly hard to accept. It is hard enough to look back on without some sense of rebellion. What must it have been to go through?

In this incident, then, it looks as if Margaret Clitherow came face to face with two things—the last lurking-place of self in her own heart, and the mystery of God's grace, which would not force her husband's choice. It was a very spiritual brand of selfishness, but selfishness nonetheless. The hidden conflict in her mind was jerked to the surface by her husband's words. She had to face the fact that she might fail in the dearest hope of her life. Anything self-regarding in that hope had now to be surrendered to God. She made that surrender.

From now on, it looks as if her inward sacrifice to God were perfect, in so far as perfection is possible to human nature. She unreservedly yielded to God all her human loves. Not that her love weakened or faltered, but she ceased to feel that it gave her claims, rights over those she loved. She still had duties towards them, which she tenderly fulfilled right up to the last. But when the call came, she dropped all into God's hands—her husband unconverted, apparently heading the wrong way; her children so young that there was no depending on their final choice. All this was put down at a word, peacefully, in fullest confidence that, if she herself loved God with her whole heart, mind, soul and strength, He would take charge of all her other loves. "I trust I am now discharged of them," she said in prison. But there was no hardness in her constancy. Her tenderness shines out to the very end.

～ Chapter V ～
"The Only Woman in the North Parts"

FATHER Mush was not the only person closely observing Margaret Clitherow during these years. The Council of the North had its eye on her as well.

In those days, York was farther from London than New York is today. For a long time past, the Kings had appointed a special body, called the Council of the North, to carry out the Royal policy in this remote region of their realm. When, therefore, it was decided to change the religion of the whole nation, this Council was a tool ready to hand. Its membership was overhauled to consist only of people who would carry out the Government's policy undeterred by mercy, justice or any such scruple.

From the report of Government agents, it is clear that the North was solidly Catholic in sentiment, though not always in outward behavior. It was the North which, in 1569, had risen to free the Queen from bad advisers who misrepresented the wishes of her subjects. In the North, then, the Government met in acutest form the difficulty it met in some degree everywhere: Englishmen were extremely reluctant to put the new laws into force against their neighbors. The change of religion had to be carried out very largely by men specially sent down by the Government for that purpose.

On the religious side, these non-local emissaries were the bishops, whose particular task it was to uproot every vestige of the Old Religion and make the people's life a burden to them until they conformed. As the North was specially recalcitrant, it was given an archbishop, Grindal, who had in London given evidence of something like a genius for persecution. At one time we find Grindal writing to Parker, Archbishop of Canterbury, complaining of "slanders" to the effect that his visitations and commissions were no better than the Spanish Inquisition. The complaint was made by a Puritan; and the Puritans were handled very gently indeed by comparison with the Catholics.

This religious pressure, however, was not enough; for the leading men of the North, in town and country, were very slow in bringing full legal pressure to bear. Extraordinary political pressure was required, partly to make the justices of the peace, the sheriffs and mayors of the towns, carry out the unpopular laws; partly to go beyond the strict law in a way local men were afraid to do. For this double purpose, the Council of the North was an ideal tool. Its members were selected for their persecuting spirit. At its head was the most hated man in the North, the Lord President, the Earl of Huntingdon. Some of its members— Meares, Cheeke and, above all, Hurleston—come into Father Mush's story.

Hurleston, indeed, appears to have taken a special interest in Margaret, for he described her as "the only woman in the north parts." He meant that she was an outstanding center of resistance to the Government's iniquitous laws, and her long immunity encouraged other women similarly to disregard the law. For Margaret managed her business so cleverly that for years they had no handle against her, save for refusing to go to church. For that she was fined and imprisoned. But not even the closest watching had hitherto produced any further evidence against her. Not that the Council was really particular about evidence. All it wanted was a colorable excuse. Her death was decided on long before there was any evidence on which to condemn her.

A few months before Margaret's arrest, something happened which affected the handling of her own case. The Government had not yet gotten a fully fledged spy system, but it was beginning to pay informers, mostly disgruntled employees who had a grudge against their employers. A gentleman named Marmaduke Bowes had for a time conformed, but he subsequently repented, was reconciled to the Church and hired a Catholic tutor for his children. The tutor, however, was a man of unsatisfactory character, who had to be dismissed. Arrested and questioned, he betrayed his employer to save himself. The Council of the North thereupon hanged Marmaduke Bowes, on no evidence but that of this tutor, a man "with a conscience saleable for sixpence, of known and notable infamy, as it was openly reported before the bench and proved against him." To make things worse, the charge against Bowes was not that of harboring priests; all he was accused of was giving a drink to a priest.

This sentence roused a perfect storm in the city. Not only common citizens inveighed against the wickedness of the sentence; one of the Assize [criminal court] judges, Judge Rhodes, expressed very strong disapproval. This naturally strengthened the feeling of the people and increased the unpopularity of the Council.

The Council decided upon a crafty revenge. They arranged that the next unpopular sentence should be passed by the Assize judges, who would thus suffer the wrath and contempt of the people. They knew very well that neither judge nor jury would dare acquit anyone whom the Government was determined to destroy; but it would be the judges, not the Council, who would have to suffer the odium of passing sentence. As it happened, the next outstanding case to come up was that of Margaret Clitherow. Hence, at her trial, one of her judges, Judge Rhodes, was in a towering temper, for he knew very well that he was being scored off [targeted]. The other, Judge Clinch, was chiefly interested in shuffling off the responsibility for her sentence on to other shoulders. Everyone knew that no one dare acquit her, yet that her condemnation would be highly unpopular.

For many years, as we said, Margaret managed so cleverly that the Council could get no handle against her. Then at last she did something which sooner or later was bound to come to light. She sent her eldest boy abroad to finish his education. This was illegal, but Margaret was determined that his whole education should be in Catholic hands. Just what was John Clitherow's part in it is not at all clear. It is possible that he agreed in order to salve his own conscience; or possibly Margaret acted without him, knowing that he could not risk a fuss, and that he was unlikely to refuse to support a child. However things were, they kept the matter quiet for two years. But Margaret always knew it could not remain hidden forever.

The Council did not always remain in York, but travelled around on its persecuting work. In the March of 1586, however, it came to York, and one of its first acts was to send for John Clitherow, to explain the absence of his son. Margaret realized that this was the beginning of the end.

The first day, however, nothing happened. John Clitherow obeyed the summons, but contrived to keep out of sight and came home unquestioned. Next day came a peremptory command to present himself. He replied that he had been there the day before, but had not put himself forward, seeing their lordships were busy. So off he went a second time—but now there was no hope of escaping notice. Margaret had guessed that he was to be gotten out of the way while the house was searched. As all her hiding places seemed to give security, she carried on quietly with the routine of the day. Mass was said, and the children went to their lessons.

Things fell out as she had foreseen. While her husband was awaiting the pleasure of the Council, the sheriffs of York arrived to search his house. The priest got safely away as Margaret had contrived, but she and her servants were detained downstairs while the upper floors were searched. No noise warned those above, and the first the tutor knew was that someone had opened the door of the schoolroom and closed it again. He went to see who it was and saw an armed man outside summoning help—as a matter of fact, the searcher thought he had caught a priest. Mr. Stapleton locked the door, skipped out through a window as arranged, and got away through another house. When the searchers burst open the schoolroom door, they found nothing but a party of children.

Had it been only the little Clitherows, they might not have gained much, for Anne and William were tough little Yorkshire tykes, who later showed their mettle. The same could be said of the neighbors' children whom Margaret had gathered to share the chance of a Catholic schooling. The records of the times show how trustworthy Catholic children mostly were.

But there was a weak spot. Rather bigger than the others was a foreign boy of about fourteen who had not been long in England. His father was English, his mother Flemish. He was probably lonely and unhappy in this strange town where dreadful things happened. All the terrible stories he had heard of the persecution in England were, he had found, quite true; if he had not witnessed the death of Marmaduke Bowes, he had witnessed the storm of popular indignation which the sentence had called forth. And now the terror was unloosed about him. The searchers quickly saw which child it would pay to bully. They stripped the luckless foreigner and threatened a flogging—and he gave way.

He showed them everything—where Mass was said and where the vestments and altar breads were kept. (Had Margaret tried to make him feel at home by letting him into the secret?) This was a haul beyond what the searchers had hoped for, clear evidence that Mass was actually said in the house in spite of the law. He told them everything he knew, and some things he didn't: as soon as he realized that these terrifying people were pleased at what he could tell, he was only too willing to speak and not too particular as to what he said.

So the house was ransacked, the searchers carrying off the hangings of two or three beds, as well as the vestments and the altar breads. Margaret's children, Anne and William, were put in the charge of Protestants and treated unkindly to make them go to church. Her servants and she were arrested, but confined separately. Margaret was never allowed to see them or her children again.

When she was brought before the Council, she astonished everyone by being not only fearless, but merry and smiling as well. Even the arrest of her husband did not quench her—she had foreseen the danger, and it may have been a relief to have the suspense end when the outcome was inevitable. The Council's fury was aroused by her demeanor, and after keeping her in court till about seven, they sent her to confinement in the Castle. An hour later, her husband was sent after her, but they were not allowed to meet. On the way to the Castle, something seems to have happened, for Margaret arrived dripping wet and had to borrow dry things for the night.

All this was on March 10, a Thursday. For two days Margaret was alone in prison. Then on that Saturday a companion was sent to her. The Council was so short of evidence against Catholics that it was working the foreign boy for all he was worth. They had long wanted a reasonable excuse to arrest Mrs. Anne Tesh, a staunch Catholic and a great friend of Margaret. (My own guess is that she played a part in Margaret's conversion and that little Anne Clitherow had been named after her.) The Council now sent for her and asked the boy if he could identify her as one of the women who went to Mass in Margaret's house. To their disappointment, he said, "No." One of them, Cheeke, exclaimed chaffingly: "Why then, this is

Mrs. Tesh, thou knowest her well enough."

"No marvel if he know me now," said Mrs. Tesh with spirit, "after you have told him who I am." They ordered the jury to bring in a verdict against her; the jury, however, would only do so for hearing Mass, not for harboring priests. Thereupon Rhodes, Hurleston and others uttered filthy abuse, declaring that they would yet have her on the capital charge. After all this, she was sent to the Castle and confined in the same cell as Margaret.

One might expect that two days of solitude had dampened Margaret's spirits, especially as she had been practicing severe abstinence ever since her arrest. Not a bit. Anne Tesh found her as merry as usual; indeed, the two seem to have had great fun together over the inconveniences of their cell—no spoons, and broken cups and plates. They were so gay that Margaret presently sobered up. "Sister," she said, "we are so merry together that, unless we be parted, I fear we shall lose the merit of our imprisonment." Another sobering thing for Margaret was an interview with her husband. This took place in the presence of the jailer. Margaret never saw him again.

Meantime, the Council was busy preparing for her condemnation. Not only had they gotten the foreign boy, they also spread rumors in the town. This spreading of rumors after an arrest was a regular part of the Government's technique; it was a sort of "war of nerves" used in the hopes that someone would lose his head and give something away. In this case, the story circulated was that Margaret had been arrested for harboring two priests, Mr. Francis Ingleby of Douay and Mr. John Mush of Rome. Father Ingleby was already in prison, but there was no evidence against him; one object was to get some tactless person to incriminate him while trying to exonerate Margaret. If someone even said: "It couldn't be Ingleby, he's in prison," the reply would be, "Oh, so you know he's a priest. Just you come and tell that to a jury." This difficulty in getting evidence shows how strong was popular sympathy on the Catholic side.

Presently, messengers were sent to tell these rumors to Margaret herself, in the hopes of startling her into saying something indiscreet. She was also told that she would suffer under the new statute, 27 Elizabeth, which had made it a hanging matter to have a priest in one's house. She laughed on hearing this and said to the messengers: "I would I had some good thing to give you for these good news. Hold, take this fig, for I have nothing better."

The hope of martyrdom brought real joy to her, so much so that she could not keep it to herself. On Monday, March 14, while she was waiting to be summoned for her trial, she exclaimed to Mrs. Tesh: "Yet before I go, I will make all my brethren and sisters on the other side of the hall merry," and looking forth from the window towards them—they were five and thirty and might easily behold her from thence—she made a pair of gallows on her fingers and pleasantly laughed at them.

This was before dinner, and it shows that up till then Margaret was expecting to be hanged, at her venerated Knavesmire, like the other martyrs of York. Yet when she was taken into court, she gave the whole proceedings a new turn, for she did something no one had foreseen and which plunged the whole city into an uproar. She refused to plead.

∾ Chapter VI ∾

Queen's Law—or God's?

SOME time after dinner on Monday, March 14, 1586, Margaret Clitherow was brought before the Assize judges in the Common Hall, now called the Guild Hall of York. One of her judges, Rhodes, was in a black fury for personal reasons, though he seems to have been a rough, almost violent man at his best. The conduct of the case was largely left to the unfortunate Judge Clinch. He hated the job, but to refuse it would be to ruin his career. He hoped to salve an uneasy conscience by at least sharing the responsibility with others. To make his position yet more uncomfortable, the Council of the North, though it intended the judges to bear the odium of the case, took steps to see that its wishes were carried out. Some members of the Council, therefore, sat on the bench with the judges, among them the infamous Hurleston, the particular enemy of Margaret.

There was a huge crowd in the streets and in the court, for Margaret was dearly loved by rich and poor alike. They had come to weep over her, and were amazed to see her not merely collected,

54

but laughing. Through all that follows, we must keep in mind this surging crowd in the background, the whole city following the case with a roar of talk, avid for every detail, crowding to catch a glimpse of her.

In court her indictment was read, that she had "harboured and maintained Jesuits and seminary priests, traitors to the Queen's majesty and her laws, and that she had heard Mass and such like." Then Judge Clinch stood up and said: "Margaret Clitherow, are you guilty of this indictment or no?" She answered quietly but with a smile: "I know of no offense whereof I should confess myself guilty!"

"Yes," said Clinch, "you have harboured and maintained Jesuits and priests, enemies of her majesty." Margaret answered, "I never knew nor have harboured any such persons [i.e., traitors], or maintained those which are not the Queen's friends. God defend [forbid] I should."

Judge Clinch may have expected this: it was the usual line of defense of accused Catholics, since after all it was a pure artifice to make priesthood the equivalent of treason. In any case, Clinch's concern was to get rid of some part of the responsibility for her death, so he passed over her reply and asked: "How will you be tried?"

At this point Margaret sprang her surprise. She replied: "Having made no offense, I need no trial." No one seems to have known what to make of this, and after badgering her for some time to take her case before a jury—called in those days "the country"—they got a further statement from her: "If you say I have offended and must be tried, I will be tried by none but God and your own consciences." This was exactly what Clinch wished to avoid—his conscience was in revolt against the whole business. So he battled with her for some time longer, reiterating: "We sit here to see justice and law, and therefore you must be tried by the country [jury]." He badly wanted those twelve men to share his blame. Margaret as badly wanted to restrict it to one man. She knew she had no chance of acquittal.

As Margaret proved obdurate, they sought to shake her in another way. They brought in two chalices, some holy pictures, the Mass vestments and the altar breads found in her house, and staged a mocking farce with them. Two low fellows dressed up in the vestments, and after some clowning, held up the altar breads, saying, "Behold thy gods in whom thou believest." Someone asked Margaret how she liked the vestments. She answered steadily, "I like them well, if they were on the backs of those that know how to use them in God's honour, as they were made."

Clinch now tried to get her to discredit herself by confessing to idolatry—or what they could twist as idolatry. He stood up again and asked: "In whom believe you?" Margaret answered: "I believe in God."

"In what God?" quoth the judge. "I believe," she replied, "in God the Father, in God the Son, and God the Holy Ghost; in these Three Persons I fully believe, and that by the passion, death and merits of Christ Jesu I must be saved." There was nothing to take hold of. "You say well," said Clinch, and sat down.

The other judges then strove to persuade her to be tried "by God and the country [jury]." As she still refused, Clinch sought to reassure her. He told her that there was no evidence against her but that of a child; therefore, she had no reason to fear a jury. On the other hand, if she persisted in her attitude, she would, he told her, "be guilty and accessory of your own death, for we cannot try you but by order of law." This suggestion that she was committing suicide, since a jury would probably acquit her—an entirely false suggestion—was used again and again to shake her resolution.

As she refused to be shaken, the next attempt was to get her to incriminate her husband. All they drew was a clear testimony that he knew nothing of what she had done. Clinch then warned her solemnly that, if she refused trial, the law would sentence her to a more painful death than a jury could. Margaret replied cheerfully: "God's will be done; I think I may suffer any death for this good cause." Her smiling face made some people think she was mad. It also made some members of the court mad. Rhodes railed at her. But it was left to Hurleston to provide the most shocking touch in all this travesty of justice. From his place on the bench, he called out in open court: "It is not for religion that thou harbourest priests, but for harlotries." This slander was industriously circulated, but made no impression on anyone who knew Margaret.

The case had come on in the afternoon and had quickly reached this deadlock. Clinch was still unwilling to act on his own responsibility. He therefore sent her back to prison for the night, hoping that reflection in the dark would alter her mind. It also gave a chance to see that she was fully informed about her position; for, so far, it looks as if Margaret had not quite understood the consequences of her action.

So she was taken back to prison, not now to the Castle and her friend Anne Tesh, but to a much worse prison built on the bridge over the river Ouse. And a Puritan preacher, Wiggington, was allowed to visit her that night. Possibly he was employed to explain to her what would happen if she still refused to plead. Possibly, too, Wiggington himself had not previously grasped the position; for the information made an unexpected impression on his own mind.

As the law then stood, anyone who refused to give evidence, or an accused person who refused to plead, was sentenced to what was called the *peine forte et dure* [literally, "strong and hard punishment"]. The person thus sentenced was laid naked on the stone floor of an underground cell with a door laid over him, and on the door, weights were piled. Originally, he was left thus for three days, during which he was given only a little bad bread and dirty water; then, if he still proved obdurate, further weights were piled on

him, until he was pressed to death. By the sixteenth century, though the old form of sentence
was pronounced, it seems to have been used only
as a method of execution, not as a way of forcing
people to testify or to plead.

When Margaret left the Castle, we saw that she
clearly expected to be hanged. She was, as she
said herself, "unskilled in your temporal laws"—
her skill was in the moral law. At this stage, then,
she was simply using her woman's wit to stave off
something she feared more than any penalty, that
her children might be forced to give evidence
against her. Nothing, she well knew, could save
her life unless she abjured her Faith. As she
would die in any case, to die in a more painful way
for the sake of her children seemed to her a very
small thing. And her mind was too clear to be
shaken by the suggestion that she would be guilty
of her own death if she refused to plead. Her
death was determined on unless she abjured, as
the court and she perfectly well knew.

Next day, Tuesday, March 15, things began
early, for Margaret was taken back to the Common Hall at eight in the morning. Clinch
addressed her with an air of concern, all the more
deceptive because it was partly sincere:
"Margaret Clitherow, how say you yet? Yester-
night we passed you over without judgment,
which we might then have pronounced against
you if we would: we did it not, hoping you would
be something conformable, and put yourself to the
country [jury]; otherwise, you must needs have

the law. We see nothing why you should refuse; here be but small witness against you, and the country will consider your case."

Margaret stripped off the camouflage and went to the heart of the offer. "Indeed," she said, "I think you have no witness against me but children, which with an apple and a rod you may make to say what you will." They then gave away their trick by reminding her of much more dangerous evidence: "It is plain that you had priests in your house by these things which were found."

The proceedings then degenerated into a wrangle as to whether Catholic priests were or were not traitors, Margaret insisting that they were "virtuous men sent by God only to save our souls," Rhodes, Hurleston and the rest declaring they were traitors.

Clinch listened awhile, then got back to what was, for him, the real point: "What say you? Will you put yourself to the country, yea or no?" Margaret said again: "I see no cause why I should do so in this matter: I refer my cause only to God and your own consciences." A clamor then broke out, for it seems to have occurred to no one that here was a mother fighting to defend her own children; their minds were full of the foreign boy. Some condemned her folly and obstinacy, others begged her to yield. Clinch again warned her that if she refused a jury, the law would punish her even more cruelly.

Suddenly an interruption occurred. Wiggington, the Puritan preacher who had visited her the night before, stood up and shouted above the clamor, demanding to be heard. But until the judge commanded silence, his voice was drowned. When at last he could make himself heard, he said: "My lord, take heed what you do. You sit here to do justice: this woman's case is touching life and death: you ought not, either by God's law or man's, to judge her to die upon the slender witness of a boy: nor unless you have two or three sufficient men of very good credit to give evidence against her. Therefore, look to it, my lord, this gear goeth sore [this is a serious business]."

Clinch answered: "I may do it by law."

Then Wiggington went to the heart of the issue. "By what law?" he asked—and indeed, the Puritans had reasons of their own for asking the question, for they too were challenging the right of the secular power to decide the religion of its subjects. Perhaps that is why Clinch answered him on a note of defiance: "By the Queen's law."

"That may well be," said the Puritan, "but you cannot do it by God's law." And having stated the issue, he pressed it no further, but sat down. Perhaps he knew it was useless to say more. Perhaps he thought—for Wiggington had a pleasing simplicity of character—that Clinch only needed to be told his duty; his conscience would do the rest.

And, indeed, Wiggington's words pricked that conscience most uncomfortably. Clinch began to renew his pleading with Margaret, but was cut short by his brother on the bench. "Why stand we all day about this naughty, willful woman?" said

Judge Rhodes. And Clinch gave way.

"If you will not put yourself to the country," he said to Margaret, "this must be your judgment:

"You must return from whence you came, and there, in the lowest part of the prison, be stripped naked, laid down, your back upon the ground, and as much weight laid upon you as you are able to bear, and so to continue three days without meat or drink, except a little barley bread and puddle water, and the third day to be pressed to death, your hands and feet tied to posts, and a sharp stone under your back."

Margaret listened to her sentence unmoved, then said quietly: "If this judgment be according to your own conscience, I pray God send a better judgment before God [i.e., may God show me greater mercy when I appear in judgment before Him]. I thank God heartily for this."

Clinch did not like the reminder of the judgment seat of God. "Nay," said he, "I do it according to law, and tell you this must be your judgment, unless you put yourself to be tried by the country. Consider of it, you have husband and children to care for; cast not yourself away." Again the suggestion that she was willfully throwing her life away when she could easily save it—one is sorry for Clinch, except when he stooped to these base expedients. Margaret answered steadily: "I would to God my husband and children might suffer with me for so good a cause." She meant, of course, that she longed they might have equal faith and constancy. But the Council had it put about that she said she would like to see her husband and children hanged.

Clinch again made clear to her that the sentence was conditional: if only she would take her case to a jury, she could expect mercy. These offers of mercy to Catholics, right to the foot of the scaffold, are in fact proof that no real crime had been committed and that at bottom the Government knew it. At any point, let us remember, Margaret could have had an easier death by agreeing to plead, and could have saved her life altogether by abjuring her religion. As she would not abjure, she knew she must die in the one way or the other; so she chose the death that most spared others.

At this offer of mercy, Margaret raised her eyes to Heaven, then said cheerfully: "God be thanked, all that He shall send me shall be welcome: I am not worthy of so good a death as this is: I have deserved death for mine offenses to God, but not for anything that I am accused of."

At the judge's direction, the sheriff then pinioned her arms with a cord, while Margaret, looking first at one arm then at the other, rejoiced to be bound for Christ's sake. She was then taken back to prison, escorted by guards armed with halberts. Observers were sent to watch how she was taking it: her happy, smiling face astonished everybody. Some said: "It must needs be that she has received comfort of the Holy Ghost." Others said, "She is possessed of a smiling devil." And the story that she was willfully taking her own life was assiduously spread through the town.

∽ Chapter VII ∽

Strife of Tongues

FOR all her smiling face, Margaret had had a shock. One detail in her sentence she had not expected—that she should be stripped naked. This troubled her more than all the rest. Even so, part of her discomfort was on the score of others. "I was ashamed on their behalfs," she said, "to have such shameful words uttered in the audience, as to strip me naked, and press me to death among men, which, me-thought, for womanhood they might have concealed."

She dealt with it very practically. Obtaining a length of linen and some tape, she busied herself making a loose garment opening down the back; its long sleeves were finished with tapes in order that there should be something ready to bind her hands at the last. The work may have helped her through difficult hours, but she was not free to give herself to it continuously. For she was never alone. Not only was she constantly harassed by Protestant ministers sent by the Council, but she was confined with a man and wife of the name of Yoward, who were in prison for debt and had been selected for their fanatical Protestantism. Mrs.

Yoward was a good-hearted creature, and Margaret entirely won her—not to the Faith but to friendship. Indeed, it is fairly clear that Mrs. Yoward was one of Father Mush's most important informants.

While Margaret herself realized that nothing could save her unless she abjured her religion, her friends had another idea: they wanted to carry the case to London and win a reprieve, if necessary from the Queen herself. The Government was very slow to execute women for their religion; even imprisoning them had made them heroines with the whole country. Only three women were actually put to death for their religion under Queen Elizabeth: Margaret Clitherow, Anne Lyne and Margaret Ward. The usual practice was to reprieve and imprison for life, rather than give them the popular appeal of martyrdom. For instance, about ten years later, Margaret's friend, Anne Tesh, converted a Protestant minister and was sentenced to be burned alive, the usual punishment for women for high treason. But she was reprieved and kept in prison till the Queen's death. And in London a certain Widow Wiseman, whom little Anne Clitherow was later to meet in her convent in Louvain, was sentenced to the same death as our Margaret. Mrs. Wiseman, however, had relations who managed to reach the ear of the Queen through some of her ladies in waiting. And when Elizabeth heard that all she was accused of was giving "a French crown" to a priest, she spared Mrs. Wiseman's life, and also sent for the judges to scold them for their cruelty. Though these events were in the future, in 1586 Margaret's friends judged rightly in thinking that they might win a reprieve if they could reach the Queen.

But London was very far off, and the Council of the North was determined to rush the execution through. The first necessity, therefore, was to secure a delay. Now, Margaret had apparently told some of her women friends that she thought she might be expecting, though she was not quite sure. It was an ancient custom that an expectant mother should never be put to death till after the birth of her innocent child. Margaret's friends, therefore, eagerly reported what she had said, in hopes of gaining time.

It raised their hopes when Judge Clinch jumped at the excuse for a delay. Consulted by the sheriffs in court, he firmly declared that on no account would he consent to her death. Judge Rhodes said, "Brother, you are too merciful in these cases: if she had not the law, she would undo a good many." One difficulty was that Margaret, questioned in prison, refused to commit herself one way or the other, as she had been mistaken before. Four women sent to examine her reported that, on the whole, they thought the diagnosis correct. Cheered by Clinch's firmness, Margaret's friends must have gone to bed in good heart. This was just two days after sentence had been pronounced.

That evening, however, a deputation waited

upon Clinch in his lodgings. It consisted of Hurleston, some other members of the Council, and several Protestant ministers. Hurleston was clearly the moving spirit. He strongly insisted that Margaret should not have the benefit of her condition. When Clinch seemed disposed to hold to his previous declaration, Hurleston said: "She is the only woman in the North Parts, and if she be suffered [allowed] to live, there will be more of her order without any fear of law. And, therefore, my lord, consider yourself, and let her have law according to the judgment passed, for I will take it upon my conscience that she is not with child." If Hurleston would take it upon his conscience, that was enough for Clinch. He had given in too often to be able to stand now. He put a good color on his surrender by holding up the execution for a week longer. That was his last effort on Margaret's behalf.

During the ten days between her sentence and her death, Margaret was not allowed to see any of her friends—officially, that is, for Elizabethan jailers were anything but "sea-green incorruptible," and it is clear that some of Margaret's friends did manage to get speech with her. What they wanted was an explanation with which to answer the slanders being spread against her in the town. The most damaging was that she "died desperately," i.e., that she was virtually a suicide. This was deeply dishonest, as no jury would have dared acquit her. And no one seems to have had the wit to see that she was fighting for her children.

"Alas," said Margaret—was she hurt that her own friends were so slow to guess her motives?— "Alas, if I had put myself to the country [jury], evidence must needs have come against me, which I know none could give but only my children and servants. And it would have been more grievous to me than a thousand deaths if I should have seen any of them brought forth before me to give evidence against me. Secondly, I know well that the country must have found me guilty to please the Council, which earnestly seek my blood; and then they had all been accessory to my death, and damnably offended God. I thought it, therefore, the way of charity on my part to hinder the country from such a sin; and since it must needs be done, to cause as few to do it as might be; and that was the judge himself."

While her own friends could contrive only hurried snatches of conversation, Margaret hardly had any respite from the ministers sent by the authorities. Here, the Council had a twofold aim. Its greatest triumph would have been her capitulation; hence, she was dragged all through the controversies of the age: the true Church, the Sacraments, invocation of Saints, and so forth. Failing in this, the second aim was to find some way of discrediting her with her fellow townsmen. She was so generally beloved that even the Council disliked incurring the unpopularlity of her death, and sought every opportunity to besmirch her character in the hope of alienating sympathy from her.

The only person who might be called a friend who was allowed to see her was her stepfather, Henry Maye, who was that year Lord Mayor of York. His wife, who was Margaret's mother, had died a few months before, and apart from that, we saw earlier that Margaret was in all probability really fond of this stepfather of hers. At least he made the strongest possible attack on her feelings. He went on his knees to her, begging her to yield. When she stood firm, he offered to take charge of her little girl. The sting of this was that the child was being ill-used to make her give up the religion in which she had been reared; Henry Maye doubtless promised to rescue her from her present guardianship and treat her kindly. And Margaret refused, preferring that Anne should suffer rather than be infected with heresy through kind treatment in her step-grandfather's household. When he had failed in all this, Henry Maye went home and diligently spread the slander that she "died desperately." As he was Lord Mayor and the only relation allowed to see her, his word must have carried weight.

The usual efforts were made to get her to admit that the priests in her house were traitors. When this failed to shake her, they fell back on the indecent suggestion shouted at her by Hurleston during her trial. They tried to make her admit that she had been unfaithful to her husband.

The foreign boy, they told her, had "confessed that she had sinned with priests, and that the priest would have delicate cheer [food] when she would set her husband with bread and butter and a red herring."

"God forgive you for these forged tales," Margaret replied, "and if the boy said so, I warrant he will say as much more for a pound of figs." They were quite capable of inventing a confession for him; indeed, a moment before she had been protesting at other lies of theirs. Finding they could not browbeat her with talk of the boy, they dropped him and pressed the accusation, urging her to confess to infidelity. Her denials only brought on fresh urging. At last she replied with spirit:

"I trust my husband will not accuse me that I have offended him at any time, except in such small matters as are commonly incident to husband and wife; and I beseech you," she added, "let me speak with him before I die." Her request was refused, but one is glad to record that her husband would never hear a word against her. Indeed, when John Clitherow learned of her condemnation, "he fared like a man out of his wits, and wept so vehemently that blood gushed out of his nose in great quantity, and said, 'Alas! Will they kill my wife? Let them take all I have and save her, for she is the best wife in all England, and the best Catholic also.'"

Most of these ministers came to entrap her. Just one came with a sincere desire to help, Wiggington, the Puritan preacher who had spoken up at her trial. Margaret seems to have recognized his sincerity and kindness of heart, for in her replies to him, there is a flicker of her old humor. The other ministers grew coarse and abusive when they could not answer her, and save for an occasional touch of irony, she answered them seriously. With Wiggington she was playful. It is a tribute to him as well as to her.

"Mrs. Clitherow, I pity your case," he led off at his first visit after her condemnation. "I am sent to see if you will be any whit conformable. Cast not yourself away. Lose not both body and soul. Possibly you think you shall have martyrdom, but you are foully deceived. . . . Not death, but the cause of death, maketh a martyr. In the time of Queen Mary, many were put to death, and now also in this Queen's time, for two several [distinct] opinions: both these cannot be martyrs. Therefore, good Mrs. Clitherow, take pity on yourself. Christ Himself fled His persecutors, and so did His Apostles: and why should you not then favour your own life?"

"God defend [forbid] I should favour my life in this point," she replied. "As for my martyrdom, I am not yet assured of it, for that I am yet living; but if I persevere to the end, I verily believe I shall be saved."

Was she gently baiting Wiggington? If so, he rose nobly to the bait, for this was a major point of the Puritan doctrines. They believed in what they called "indefectible grace": that grace once given could never be lost. Anyone who had once received grace would be assured of the fact, and after that could never fall away.

"Are you not assured?" he asked eagerly.

"No, I wis [think, suppose]," replied she, "so long as I am living, because I know not what I may do."

Wiggington seems to have been puzzled. His ideas of Catholic doctrine had probably all been derived from Protestant sources, and he was thrown out of his stride on meeting the reality. At any rate, instead of following up the question of grace and free will, he went off at a tangent: "How think you, Mrs. Clitherow, to be saved?"

"Through Christ Jesu, His bitter passion and death," she replied.

"You say well," he said, "but you believe far otherwise, as in images, Sacraments, sacramentals, and such like, not only in Christ."

Margaret patiently explained the Catholic doctrine: "I believe," she said, "as the Catholic Church teacheth me, that there be Seven Sacraments, and in this faith I will both live and die. As for all the ceremonies, I believe they be ordained to God's honour and glory, and the setting forth of His glory and service; as for images, they be but to represent unto us that there were both good and godly men upon earth, which are now glorious in Heaven, and also to stir up our dull minds to more devotion when we behold them; otherwise than this, I believe not."

After arguing about how many Sacraments there are, Wiggington said mildly (where other ministers would have lost their temper): "Well, Mrs. Clitherow, I am sorry that I cannot persuade you," and went away.

He returned some days later. Margaret must have been dog-weary by now, as she had had little food and little rest since her condemnation. Perhaps Wiggington's kindness had a tonic effect; except for Mrs. Yoward, he was the only truly kind person she met through all those trying days. At any rate, she was charmingly playful with him. His intention this time was to persuade her to go to church and hear a sermon, which would have been accepted as an official act of abjuration. Margaret—was he not warned by a twinkle in her eye?—answered demurely, "I will with all my heart hear a sermon." He was beginning to be delighted, but she cut in: "I pray you, understand me: I mind [intend] to do it, if I may have a Catholic priest or preacher, but to come to your sermons will I never."

Wiggington ploughed on: "If you will come to a sermon," he promised, "I shall procure you a good and godly man both of life and doctrine, though I seek him in the furthermost part of England." This was a very necessary assurance, for at that time the credit of the Protestant clergy stood low. The type of clergy we now associate with the Church of England hardly began to appear for another generation.

Mrs. Yoward seems to have been keenly following the discussion, for she now burst in: "Here is the Dean of Durham, Toby Matthew, a godly and learned man: I am sure he will take as much pains as any other to do you good." Mrs. Yoward had excellent taste. Dean Matthew was quite one

of the best of the Elizabethan clergy, a sincere
man of good life, with a real pastoral care for his
flock, markedly different from the avaricious
bishops who earned from the Puritans the nick-
name of "bitesheep." He later became Archbishop
of York, and his real goodness was rewarded in a
way which perhaps he did not fully appreciate:
his son, also Sir Toby Matthew, became a
Catholic. Indeed, it was he who put out those
twenty-four reasons for becoming a Catholic to
which we alluded when talking of Margaret's own
conversion (p. 7).

Margaret, however, refused even the virtuous
Dean of Durham. "My faith is already stayed," she
said, "and I purpose not to seek for any new
doctrines."

Wiggington then played what he hoped was his
trump card. "I myself," he told her, "have seen
Christ once in a vision." Margaret was so amused
that she could hardly keep from laughing. Disap-
pointed of the effect he had hoped to produce,
Wiggington fell back on passages from the Doctors of the Church.

Margaret spoke up firmly. "If you would believe
the Doctors and follow them, then were both you
and I of one Faith, but you slide from them. I have
no learning to read them, but I believe that which
they preached and taught to be the truth." Wiggington was the only person of whom Margaret
remotely suggested that it was possible they could
ever be joined in the fellowship of faith—it was a
tribute to him, but not one he could appreciate.

"Well, Mrs. Clitherow," he said, keeping his temper but allowing himself one little stab, "I perceive you will cast yourself willingly [willfully] away, without regard for your husband and children; you follow blind guides. Is there any of them that hath learning, I would fain know."

"Peruse their works and see," answered Margaret shortly. The suggestion that she was without affection for her husband and children dried up her laughter. Wiggington stood pitying her for some time longer, then took himself off. He had the good feeling to stay away, realizing that he could accomplish nothing.

The most cruel of all the charges made against Margaret was that she had no regard for her husband and children. It drew from her one of her noblest declarations. "You charge me wrongfully," she said to a minister far less scrupulous than Wiggington. "I do not die desperately nor willingly procure my own death; for not being guilty of such crimes as were laid against me, and yet condemned to die, I could but rejoice, my cause being also God's quarrel. . . . As for my husband, know you that I love him next unto God in this world, and I have care over my children as a mother ought to have: I trust I have done my duty to them to bring them up in the fear of God, and so I trust I am now discharged of them. And for this cause I am willing to offer them freely to God that sent them [to] me, rather than I will yield one jot of my Faith. I confess death is fearful, and flesh is frail: yet I mind [intend] by God's assistance to spend my blood in this Faith, as willingly as ever I put my paps to my children's mouths, neither desire I to have my death deferred. . . . I take witness I die for the Catholic Faith, the same that I was christened in."

"What is the Church?" they had asked her bullyingly at an earlier interview, and she replied: "It is that wherein the true word of God is preached, which Christ left to His Apostles, and to their successors ministering the Seven Sacraments, which the same Church hath always observed, the Doctors preached, and martyrs and confessors witnessed. This is the Church I believe to be true. . . . I beseech you, trouble me not. I am no divine, neither can I answer these hard questions. I am according to the Queen's majesty's laws to die, and my spirit is willing, although my flesh may repine. I say, as I have said heretofore, my desire is to die a member of the Catholic Church. My cause is God's, and it is a great comfort to me to die in His quarrel: flesh is frail, but I trust in my Lord Jesu, that He will give me strength to bear all troubles and torments which shall be laid upon me for His sake."

Chapter VIII

Crown of Martyrdom

MARGARET's friends, of course, could not know what was going on behind the scenes, the consultations between judges, Council, sheriffs and so forth. But if they had cherished hopes that their plans for a delay had succeeded, those hopes were dashed for good when her husband was set free but ordered to leave the city for some days. Everyone realized that he was being gotten out of the way during the execution.

Margaret herself had never expected any other end—unless she apostatized. In her humility, she always knew that this remained a possibility; she never vaunted her own constancy, but prayed God's grace to keep her from falling. We, looking back after four hundred years, may marvel at her steadfastness. She herself, living minute by minute through those terrible ten days, felt herself shaking and shaken in mind and body. From the outside, we can see that it was just this sense of her weakness which was her real strength, for it drove her to put all her trust in God. From the inside, what she herself was aware of was her own quailing insufficiency.

Besides the insistent onslaught on her firmness of mind—promises, threats, slanders, the love of husband and children—Margaret had to reckon with the fierce desire for life of her young, beautiful body. She was intensely alive, vital, vivid, a woman in the prime of her strength, bound to this world by all the chains of life. Death seemed to have no lot in her; all her youth and vitality cried out against it. It cannot surprise us that she was sometimes overwhelmed with fear; rather, the surprise is that she should have had only phases of collapse, against hours when she seemed her usual self, cheerful, practical, ready to joke, self-possessed and resolute.

All this clamor of her nature Margaret fought with fasting. From the day of her condemnation "her diet was a water potage, rye bread, and small ale, which she took but once a day and that in little quantity." And after the sheriffs came to tell her that in two more days she must die, she took no further food at all. Yet all the time she was being pestered by ministers, involved in arguments which might have worn down a well-fed person.

Various small indications show how carefully she had thought over the manner of her death, as if she did not wish to be again surprised by some unexpected detail. When the sheriffs came to announce the time of her death, she asked to be allowed to spend half a day or half a night beforehand in the place of her execution, presumably to accustom her mind to it. This was refused.

When they had gone, she turned to a friend and said: "The sheriffs have told me that I shall die on Friday next; and now I feel the frailty of mine own flesh, which trembleth greatly at these news, although my spirit greatly rejoiceth. Therefore for God's sake pray for me, and desire all good folk to do the same." She herself then knelt down, and "praying a little, the fear and horror of death presently [immediately] departed, as she said herself."

After that, she made her final arrangements very quietly. She had already rid herself of all merely ornamental clothing, and wore only a very plain gown. The linen robe to die in was taking shape in her hands; it was during her last three days that she mostly sewed at it. She was not allowed to see those she loved best, but to two of them she contrived to send a token. To her husband she sent her "hat"—that bonnet-like head-dress we see in portraits of the period, which a married woman wore indoors as well as out. It was the sign that she was under the authority of a husband, and Margaret sent it to John Clitherow "in sign of her loving duty to him as to her head." Her shoes and stockings she sent to poor little Anne, then twelve years old, "signifying that she should serve God and follow in her steps." Anne took the hint. John Clitherow, though heart-broken at the time, made no change that we can detect in the direction of his life.

On the last night, Thursday, March 24, Margaret was overcome with an intense longing for the presence of someone she knew, if only one of her devoted servants. She spoke of this to Mrs. Yoward, "not for any fear of death, for it is my comfort, but the flesh is frail." Mrs. Yoward had clearly become very fond of Margaret. "Alas, Mrs. Clitherow," said she, "the gaoler [jailer] is gone, the door is locked, and none can be had." Mrs. Yoward did her best to fill the gap. Though she was ready for bed, she put on her clothes again and sat with Margaret on the bed, for there was no other seat. But for all her good will, she grew more and more sleepy; so that in the end Margaret passed through her Gethsemane alone.

From time to time, Mrs. Yoward roused up enough to see what was happening. At midnight she opened her eyes and saw Margaret do something very strange. She got up, took off her clothes, and dressed herself in the long linen robe she had made for her death. In the cold of a March night, she knelt thus lightly clad on the floor, and so remained for several hours. About three in the morning, her movements again aroused Mrs. Yoward, who saw her get up, walk over to the fireplace, and there lie down on the cold stones of the hearth. In the wooden floored room, those were the only stones available. On them Margaret lay on her back for about a quarter of an hour. Was she rehearsing her death? For so she would lie on the stone floor of the Toll Booth where she was to die. After a quarter of an hour, she rose from the hearth and went to bed, pulling clothes over her. And as far as Mrs.

Yoward knew, there she remained until six o'clock, when she got up and dressed.

To Mrs. Yoward's surprise, the depression and fear of the night had completely passed away. Yet Margaret's mind was still busy with the details of her death. She told Mrs. Yoward how she wished some Catholic could be present to pray for her; and then, as that was impossible, suggested that the good soul might come herself and remind her of God in her agony. This was more than Mrs. Yoward could stand. She protested vehemently that "she would not see her die so cruel a death for all York," and then had a bright idea: "I will procure some friends," said she, "to lay weight on you that you may be quickly despatched from your pain." "Procure" in prison language simply meant "bribe." Margaret would not have it. "No, good Mrs. Yoward, not so," said she. "God forbid that I should procure any to be guilty of my death and blood."

At eight, when the sheriffs came, they found her ready. Since she had sent her "hat" to her husband, her bright brown hair had to be tied up somehow. She simply used the tape left over from her sewing. With her gown cast loosely about her, her feet and legs bare, she set out with the sheriffs, carrying the linen robe over her arm.

There was such a crowd in the street that they could hardly get by. One of the sheriffs, Gibson, loathed the job and tried to be as considerate as possible. The other, Fawcet, was a surly man who wanted to hustle her along. Did she remember the days when her own father had been sheriff of York, and had left money to the poor of the city to pray for his soul? She carefully observed the forms proper in speaking to city dignitaries: "Good Master Sheriff, let me deal my poor alms before I now go, for my time is short." All marvelled at her joyous looks.

They had only six or seven yards to go from the prison on the Ousebridge to the Toll Booth, where she was to die. Besides Gibson and Fawcet, who were in charge of the execution, there went in with her the following: a minister so rough and hectoring that even Protestants sometimes refused to go to his church; a kinsman of Cheeke, and another of his creatures—possibly members of the Council did not trouble to get up so early in the morning; four sergeants who ought to have carried out the execution but who liked the job so little that they had hired four beggars to do it for them; three or four more men; and four women.

In the Toll Booth, Margaret knelt down to pray. Even now they could not leave her in peace, but— after all that had happened!—bade her pray and they would pray with her. To consent would have been taken as a surrender of all for which she was giving her life. It was no time to mince words, so she answered roundly: "I will not pray with you, nor shall you pray with me: neither will I say Amen to your prayers, nor shall you to mine." What fellowship has light with darkness? Anything else would have been an acted lie.

But while Margaret would compromise no principle, she was careful to obey every command where obedience was possible. When they ordered her to pray for the Queen, she felt it necessary to make her position very clear. So she began to pray aloud, first for the Catholic Church, the Pope and Cardinals, then for all Christian princes. At this they interrupted her: Do not put her Majesty among that company. Margaret went steadily on: "—and especially for Elizabeth, Queen of England, that God turn her to the Catholic Faith, and after this mortal life she may receive the blessed joy of Heaven. For I wish as much good," she explained, "to her Majesty's soul as to my own."

Sheriff Gibson stood weeping at the door, but Fawcet was made of sterner stuff. "Mrs. Clitherow," he said, "you must remember and confess that you die for treason." That was the one time Margaret raised her voice; it was the heart and core of the whole quarrel. Hitherto she had spoken very quietly though very firmly. Now she cried aloud:

"No, no, Mr. Sheriff, I die for the love of my Lord Jesu!"

Fawcet then ordered her to undress, "for you must die naked as judgment was pronounced against you." Not only Margaret but all the other women went on their knees, begging him to let her keep her shift, but all that he would agree to was that the women might undress her while the men looked away.

So the women removed her clothes and put on her the long linen robe. Then very quietly she lay down on the floor, with handkerchief over her face, and the linen robe pulled down as far over her as it would go. As she lay there with her hands folded in prayer, a sharp stone the size of a man's fist was placed under her back, and a door was laid over her, covering her from sight. At this point Fawcet again intervened. "Nay, you must have your hands bound," he said. Instantly her hands, still folded in prayer, appeared above the top of the door. Two of the sergeants parted them, and with the strings of tape which she had herself provided, bound them to two stakes in the floor, so that she lay with arms outstretched in the form of a cross.

Even now they could not leave her alone. They badgered her to ask the Queen's forgiveness, and to pray for her. Margaret ignored the point about forgiveness—had she not all along maintained that she had committed no offense against the Queen? "I have prayed for her," she answered shortly. Then for the last time they struck at the most tender spot of all, bidding her ask pardon of her husband. She said simply, "If ever I offended him, but for my conscience, I ask him forgiveness."

Only then did the four hired beggars begin to lay the weights upon her. As she felt them, she was heard to say, "Jesu! Jesu! Jesu! have mercy on me!" After that, no further sound was heard but the crash of the weights, "seven or eight hundred-weight at the least." She was about a quarter of an hour dying, and the watchers stood round waiting while a pool of blood formed on the floor.

The sheriffs left the body under the door from nine in the morning until three in the afternoon. They were somewhat at a loss what to do with it, but decided at last to bury it after dark in some waste ground, where they hoped it would never be found, or at least identified.

What then happened is told us in two anonymous documents, one of which may be by Father Mush himself. The two accounts differ in details, but the main outline seems to be this. Margaret Clitherow was buried secretly in a "filthy place" or "dunghill," which six weeks later some Catholics succeeded in locating. By then, May was coming on with its short hours of darkness. By waiting for a stormy night they were able to open the grave without interference. To their surprise, as Father Mush reports, the body was still incorrupt, though terribly mangled. One of them conveyed it away "a great journey," and after six days was astonished to find it still fresh. It was, however, decided to embalm it, and a second burial took place a fortnight after the disinterment.[1] Where it was then laid was a secret so carefully guarded that it is now lost. Some time during these proceedings, a hand was detached, which is now one of the most precious treasures of the Bar Convent in York. The crisped fingers still bear eloquent testimony to the anguish of her death.

---

1. The two accounts from which these details are taken are both printed by Fr. J. Morris, S.J., in the Third Series of *Troubles of Our Catholic Forefathers*. One will be found on p. 52, the other on p. 99.

After railing fiercely against her persecutors, Father Mush finishes his story with a prayer to the martyr with which we may also end:

"But now, O Sacred Martyr, letting go thy enemies, I turn to thee. Remember me, I beseech thy perfect charity, whom thou has left miserable behind thee, in time past thy unworthy Father, and now thy most unworthy servant, made ever joyful by thy virtuous life, and comfortable by lamenting thy death; lamenting thy absence, yet rejoicing in thy glory. . . . Be not wanting, therefore, glorious Mother, in the perfection of thy charity, which was not little towards me in thy mortality, to obtain mercy and procure the plenties of such graces for me, thy miserable son, as thou knowest to be most needful for me, and acceptable in the sight of Our Lord, which hath thus glorified thee; that I may honour Him by imitation of thy happy life, and by any death which He will give me, to be partaker with thee and all holy saints of His kingdom, to whom be all honour and glory, now and for ever. Amen."

Epilogue*

Margaret Clitherow was canonized by Pope Paul VI in 1970 as one of the Forty Martyrs of England and Wales.

In the new calendar (1970), the feast of the Forty Martyrs of England and Wales is observed on October 25. Prior to the canonization of the Forty Martyrs of England and Wales, a feast of Blessed Margaret Clitherow was observed in some places on March 26.

---

*Added by the Publisher in 2003.

If you have enjoyed this book, consider making your next selection from among the following . . .

At your Bookdealer or direct from the Publisher.
Toll Free 1-800-437-5876   *www.tanbooks.com*

Prices subject to change.